LC SLOK

Y0-BDK-000

Unde

Understanding Loneliness

EDGAR N. JACKSON

FORTRESS PRESS   Philadelphia

Copyright © 1980 by Edgar N. Jackson

First Fortress Press Edition 1981

Published in the United Kingdom by SCM Press, London

———————

Library of Congress Cataloging in Publication Data

Jackson, Edgar Newman.
  Understanding loneliness.

  Includes bibliographical references.
  1. Loneliness. 2. Christian life — 1960-
I. Title.
BF575.L7J26 1981   158'.2   81–43071
ISBN 0–8006–1606–5

———————

9004D81 Printed in the United States of America 1–1606

Contents

To J W J

Solitude can be a welcome thing —
Discovering cool oases in the crowd,
Or looking up to see an eagle's wing
When every other praying head is bowed;
Exploring echo chambers of the mind
To hear again words the beloved said,
Or suddenly in frigid darkness find
The hidden drought where dying fires are fed.

But loneliness! To grope with weightless hands
Through space, a charred and orphaned satellite
Beyond the pull of sweet meridians
Where once the North Star verified the night!
To be alone means just the voice is mute,
But loneliness of soul is absolute.

by M F D

Introduction

Since I set out to write this book I have made an extensive study of the books that have been written in recent years on the subject of loneliness. I found that they fell into three categories. First were the books that treated loneliness in rather superficial form, assessing its meaning primarily as getting out of circulation; the solution was to get back into circulation again. The suggestions made were simplistic, like joining a Senior Citizen's Club, attending church or participating in a hobby group. None of these suggestions are unfortunate. They are just inadequate for understanding the large and painful problem of loneliness today.

Second were the books that recognized how painful a problem loneliness might be, but made no effort to probe to the roots of the problem, to understand its meaning. So the suggestions for resolving the problem, though well meaning, tended to be superficial and left the basic problem untouched.

The third group of books made a careful study of the impact of loneliness from the point of view of psychology, medicine and social studies. They recognized the severe nature of the problem but usually failed to move beyond diagnosis and prognosis to prescription.

In this book I shall approach loneliness from a broader perspective. While all loneliness must start in the emotions of an individual, we should recognize that it is not a simple emotion, but in its complexity emerges from past life-experience, social patterns and often obscured environmental factors. We should also see it as having a major impact on health, group life and personality development. We should even see some of the developments in religion and social disturbance as the acting out of the diffused and disturbing influence of the social epidemic of loneliness.

I want to explore the careful scientific studies that have been made to reveal the impact of loneliness, as well as the need to take corrective action against its destructive influence. I feel that different kinds of loneliness call for different types of therapeutic intervention. In order to make a clear distinction between the different kinds of loneliness I have classified them according to the cause-effect processes at work in their varied forms of development.

I shall make it clear that developmental loneliness has been ingrained in the personality by shortcomings in the early evolving of the individual. Fear, distrust, successive experiences of abandonment have often produced a self-image and a social relationship that uses loneliness as a safe retreat from more pain and injury. If there is to be any cure, it is necessary to look for the causes of loneliness and make an effort to work through unproductive social behaviour. It is then possible to create new forms of social adjustment where loneliness is not needed, and retreat and isolation are understood for what they are: non-productive behaviour and unnecessary defences.

I have classified another form of loneliness as that which emerges from triggering circumstances. These may be the result of death, moving to a strange community, becoming separated from the familiar ways of life. This circumstantial loneliness may disrupt human relations, and if there are flaws in the developmental processes of the personality it will surely compound the problems. But here changes in circumstances can usually bring about changes in the loneliness and its impact on life.

The third classification I make has to do with what I call existential loneliness. This seems to be rooted in the nature of human consciousness and the limited forms of communication that are so much a part of our human experience. Here the solution seems to be not so much a change in development or circumstance as a change in the attitude a person has towards ultimate reality, the cosmic process or the essential religious perception by which one seeks to discover an undergirding trust that sustains life even in the face of its frustrations.

I shall try to abstract from research in several areas of the personality sciences the pertinent insights that can help us understand how devastating loneliness can be personally, physically, socially and emotionally. So I am especially thankful for the careful studies made in recent years which clarify and verify the feelings so many people have had about the impact of loneliness in their lives.

I shall try to explore the personal components of life that can become the stepping stones for climbing out of the slough of despond and the pains of loneliness. I see these as a capacity for creating meaningful intimacy in healthful relations with others, not restrained by fear and distrust, but rather implemented by warmth, understanding and a desire to move towards people with confidence.

In addition to intimacy I shall explore the meaning of identity, the clear knowledge of who we are. This seems to be basic to our task, for without identity there is not a real and secure person to share in life-satisfying intimacy. I shall look at the ways in which identity is fractured, and also at the ways in which identity is confirmed, assured and restored.

I shall also look at the ways in which a person can find inner security through the processes by which inner strength and self-confidence can be built. I shall explore some of the ways in which an individual can confront loneliness, and change it into a creative experience of self-discovery in cherished times of aloneness. I shall look at ways of relating to things and people, past and present, that can be a source of growth and inspiration.

There are some things I shall not do. I shall not give the glib response that by following this or that simple formula one can get over being lonely. I do not believe that is true. Often the causes of loneliness are in the person who projects a toxic atmosphere of selfishness, hypersensitivity and poorly integrated personal needs and resources. Here there is a need for strenuous and sometimes painful reassessment, for the causes of loneliness are more likely to be in the person than in the externals of life.

I shall not suggest that some simple device in social contact will quickly solve problems of loneliness. While it is true that joining a church may provide friends and social contacts, the person determines whether the change in circumstances will be allowed to satisfy inner needs, or whether it will become yet another source of stress and frustration. People carry their inner needs about with them, and it takes more than geography and magic to produce significant changes.

I cannot promise that some superficial religious change will resolve the problems of loneliness. Instead I shall try to make it clear that a mature and sensitive relationship to the God of ultimate reality will change the focus from trying to remake other people to a clearer concept of responsibility for change in attitude and social behaviour. I want to encourage the confronting of reality with the kind of maturity that can reduce the frustrations that grow from childish ideas of cause-effect relationships. I shall suggest forms of self-discipline that know how to respect and trust the laws of nature and human nature, rather than flaunt them and then blame God if we break ourselves on the laws that are designed to provide us with unending security.

I realize that some of the tasks in personal reorientation essential to managing loneliness are not easy. So I have tried to provide some of the resources and inspiration that can make the tasks more easily comprehensible and more surely accomplishable. To that end I have used personal illustrations throughout. I trust that they will seem to be authentic, coming from the lives of real people. I am thankful to the many people who through the years have shared with me their varied experiences of loneliness. If any of them read this book, they may be sure that any personal experiences recounted in the pages that follow have been so modified that even they would not recognize them. Yet the human dynamics have been preserved so that they may illuminate the feelings and thus be a help to others.

Sometimes the illustrations came in unexpected places, for loneliness does not always wait for formal counselling. Let me give one instance. One day in the hospital I had occasion to check something with the lab technician. I had known her casually for several years. She did not seem too busy and so we drifted into conversation. I had visited several patients, seriously ill and obviously suffering quite some discomfort. I said something about suffering and enlarged on it, mentioning how hard it must be to be so aware of human suffering constantly.

My technician acquaintance responded in a way I had hardly expected. She said, 'Maybe it is because I feel depressed today, but I feel suffering of the body may not be the worst kind of suffering.'

I accepted the idea and indicated a willingness to explore it further with her. I said, 'What do you mean?'

I can only give part of her lengthy response. She said,

'No one knows what it is like down here. I am so far away from everything and everybody. Like in a dungeon. I work here all day with my beakers and test-tubes, centrifuge and chemicals. Sometimes I get so lonely I could scream. And when I get out of here sometimes I think it's worse. I don't think there is a human being on earth who cares what happens to me from five on Friday to nine on Monday. I go into my own little empty world and suffer. You know, I once thought this would be a great life – living on the frontiers of medical science, making my contribution to health and happiness. But for twenty years I have been a specialist in sputum, mucus, smears, urine and faeces. Blood, yes, not so bad. The romance of medical research – long gone. This lonely, stinking place – now my whole life stinks and I am trapped. No family, no future, no past really, just these four walls. I was all for a career and this seemed like a good one. I was over-sold. Now what do I have? No choices – this job or starvation. You don't know how miserable I am, how I suffer, how this unending lone-liness eats away at my life. Yes, upstairs they can get shots and pills and someone to hold their hand. This is the underworld and I'm stuck in it.'

This unexpected explosion of deep feeling was an authentic expression of loneliness, and it gave clues to its nature and origin. A competent, attractive professional woman was suf-fering deeply. As is so often the case with loneliness, it exists where we might not expect to find it. People seem defence-less against it.

This episode reminded me of another. This was a group counselling session I had with some nuns and priests who were trying to deepen their understanding of the human predicament. We went on for hours saying the things people usually say when they are trying to move towards their deep-est feelings. A middle-aged nun sat quietly for hours lis-tening to all that was said. Then she commented,

You may not know it, but I am going through a special kind of death. You priests will never know what it is like. I was a teenager when I thought being the bride of Christ was the most important thing in the world. I've given nearly thirty years to the church. But now I am in menopause. I know I will never be able to be what God really wanted me to be. I want a baby. I want to hold it against my breast and love it. I want a baby all my own. I hear you talk about abortion and I have trouble understanding it. We abort motherhood in the lives of thousands like me. I feel so empty, so alone, so dead inside.

And she burst into quiet sobbing. No one said anything for a long time, and a couple of her colleagues moved closer to hold her hand. Here was the depth of loneliness crying out in despair.

Amidst many social changes, there are life-styles that have revolutionary meanings for contemporary men and women. There are also some deep and abiding needs that must be confronted not only for comfort and convenience, but for matters of life and death. Not only are there changing roles for men and women, but there are also essential depths of being that have to be kept in focus. A contemporary woman author writes,

'We're very biological animals. We always tend to think that if one is in a violent state of emotional need, it is our unique emotional need or state, when it is probably just the emotions of a young woman whose body is demanding that she have children . . . who are conditioned to be one way and are trying to be another. I know lots of girls who don't want to get married or have children. And very vocal they are about it. Well, they're trying to cheat on their biology.[1]

Successful men fail to enjoy their success and move into depression, the most common form of emotional illness. Business, the military and the church face the breakdowns that come from isolation, retreat from life, bitter loneliness. And it is difficult to find people who want to talk about it because it may be too close to where they live and feel.

This book is for those who want to talk and think creatively about their experience of loneliness, not in a trivial, light-hearted way, but with an earnest effort to know what it is that is happening to them, and why it has assumed epidemic proportions in our society. I shall explore ways of coping with the developmental, circumstantial and existential forces that are creating more and more loneliness among us.

I shall not stop there. I shall try to go to the roots of the problem in understanding why there is a crisis in intimacy, in identity and in security. I shall try to understand how we can take a positive stance against the destructive impact of loneliness. I shall try to discover how we can grow in responsibility for our own destiny, and in competence in managing our failures in communication and relationship.

I shall try to discover positive ways for developing life-sustaining intimacy, true identity and a security within that can make life safe for the living. I shall look at the special life-situations that cause separation, isolation and loneliness and try to find how we can enjoy being alone as a source of creative activity and inner growth. This is not a book of easy nostrums or superficial explorations. Loneliness is not a trivial state of being, and the resolution of it is not trifling or unimportant.

This is a book that I hope will help provide resources for coping with loneliness whenever it enters life, now and in the future. We know that loneliness is painful, but we also know that much loneliness is self-inflicted punishment or a retreat from the obligations of life. If when you feel most lonely you work to reduce the loneliness of another, you may find that your own feelings of isolation and separation fade away. Loneliness often carries with it a feeling of helplessness, and the way to move beyond helplessness is to take control over some of the minor details of life.

Loneliness is always personal. Ultimately the answers to the problems of loneliness are not found in a formula so much as in fortitude; in frenzied seeking so much as in quiet solitude; in forcing fate so much as in trusting faith; in compelling life so much as in giving love. The poet finds the answer in a mood of prayer which is the source of ultimate awareness of inner resources, of the sensitive approach to the needs of others and the basic language for expressing our need for a cosmic security in life.

Today I seek to be aware,
To see the pain in shielded eyes,
To hear the beat of worried hearts,
To share with joy a child's first look
And know the weary watch of age.

To feel the quiet despair of one
Whose reach has gone beyond his grasp,
And share the deep corrosive fears
Which hide behind the lying walls
Which people build around themselves.

To shade the dazzling ego's shine
Which blurs the vision of the world.
To know with joy a moment's glance
Into the closely guarded heart
And for a moment be a friend.

Today I ask to be aware.
May I, dear Lord, have strength to stand
If to the brashness of my quest
You yield and grant me what I ask.[2]

1

What Loneliness Feels Like

One of the problems that comes with emotional distress is the trouble of finding a way to bring the feelings into sharp focus. Often the feelings are so indefinite and all-pervasive that we do not identify them properly. Many conditions that are really the product of loneliness are thought of in terms of emotional illness, depression or human failure.

So let us take some time to look at samples of loneliness, so that we can make sure we have clearly in mind what it is we are talking about. What does loneliness look like in other people? What does it feel like within ourselves? In these vignettes of lonely people we will not be interested in resolving the problems they faced. That will come later. For now, all we want to do is to get a picture of some people who might be our friends and neighbours having a Robinson Crusoe experience in a different setting.

William was a young teenager, rather bookish and ordinary looking. I was called by his parents because at that time I was serving as head of a psychiatric clinic for children and adolescents. They said they were alarmed by his behaviour and wondered what to do about it.

When I enquired about the behaviour that disturbed them, they said that he spent most of his time in his room with the door closed, playing records interminably. When they tried to engage him in conversation he was either silent or curt in his responses. They said that they felt he was unhappy, and he was certainly making them unhappy. They agreed that he was an intelligent lad whose work at school had been excellent, but that recently his grades had been slipping downwards. They wanted a professional assessment of William's behaviour, and recommendations as to what could be done to make what they felt were necessary changes.

Because William did not want to go anywhere, and was especially apprehensive about 'shrinks', I arranged to visit him in his room. He was distant and reserved in his manner. While he was not overtly hostile, he did not act as if he considered the visit a blessing. He had excellent equipment and a large collection of classical records. In response to my queries about his musical interests, he immediately became more animated, and asked if I liked Maria Callas. When I expressed appreciation for her voice and her dramatic interpretations, he opened up with an in-depth interpretation of some of her roles in opera, and asked if I wanted to hear a special recording he had recently bought. For nearly two hours we talked about Maria Callas, her life, her music and her spirit. There was no restraint in his communication, and I began to get a picture of what was happening inside him.

While I looked for the usual signs of disorientation and emotional abnormalities, and tried to pay attention to his speech and general attitudes, I was especially aware of his desire to relate and communicate about the things that interested him. During the first session there was no effort to talk with him about anything that distressed his parents. Rather, it was a time for entering into his life, his interests and enthusiasms.

When I invited him to return the visit and share some of my musical interests, he was more than willing. Enough time was set aside so that we could not only listen to music but also talk about its emotional meaning. I was interested in sharing an especially stirring and perceptive interpretation of the slow movement of Beethoven's Ninth Symphony. We explored the meaning of Beethoven's loneliness and his courage, his ability to change his despair into great acts of creativity. Finally William expressed the idea that a person had to know real loneliness to understand the true nature of Beethoven.

When we began to explore the meaning of his observation, he moved into his internal climate. He said that no one in his school seemed to appreciate good music. He spoke of the garbage they spend good money on, when they could have great music instead. It was then that we explored how values emerge, and the subtle ways that our human relations are

2

directed by our inner needs. Before long he was talking about his own loneliness and the despair that went with it. This involved some jealousy of the people who seemed to be succeeding in their friendships. Then he seemed to have a new perception of his retreat into music.

Before long we were talking about the ways in which music could be used to build bridges towards other people, rather than as a retreat into a secluded world of unreal relationships. We talked about creative performance in addition to creative listening. We tried to find out what instrument might be most easily learned and needed in the school orchestra. We fixed our efforts on the *cor anglais*, a unique instrument that may be mastered quite quickly, at least for the musical scores that were likely to be used in school orchestras. In a short time William was quite as enthusiastic about his ability to perform with others as he was anxious to retreat from others.

Teenagers are in a state of normal neurosis, with rapidly changing glandular structures and all the internal and external manifestations of that stressful condition. The social structures of in-groups and out-groups are powerful with adolescents. Once the feelings of being excluded take root in consciousness, it may seem impossible to break out of the loneliness that comes with social ostracism. When the loneliness causes withdrawal, an enlarging circle of stresses further drives a person into isolation. These conditions can impair life for long periods of time with deep misery. The need for a change in direction is indicated, and sometimes help is needed to break through the self-judgments that drive a person further and further into the lonely self.

Not all teenage problems are as easily resolved as William's. However, it can be characteristic of the age that loneliness is a painful experience that can be compounded by parental admonitions to be more like the others. The need to understand the pain of loneliness and set up some valid ways for moving beyond it with outside help may be essential to the wise management of this form of separation anxiety.

Mildred had to deal with quite a different set of conditions that produced her loneliness. Mildred was a mature and competent woman. Her professional role as a psychologist gave her a background for understanding emotions and their

3

varied manifestations. When her husband became ill and after a few months' illness died, she appeared to manage the process of her grieving with wisdom and grace.

It was more than two years later that I talked with her about her experience. She was quite candid about all the feelings that had broken loose in her life. She said that she knew all about the dynamics of grief intellectually, and understood what was happening to her well enough to take a defensive stance against the more distressing aspects of her grief. She said that she had learned to accept help when she needed it. She said that she had deepened her philosophical perceptions about life and death. She even admitted that she had become more religious and actively nurtured her faith.

In many ways Mildred testified to her strength in coping with one of life's more difficult crises. Then after quite a long pause she looked at me and said, 'But you know, the one thing I can't seem to get over is the loneliness. No one ever told me it would be like this. I keep thinking that it will subside and fade away, but it doesn't. It is as real now as it was at the beginning. I can't understand it and I have difficulty coping with it. Oh, I know all the book answers. I've read a dozen books on loneliness and how to pull oneself out of it.'

We talked for a while about the things she had tried to do. She had her family in for visits regularly and she did enjoy her children and grandchildren. But she admitted that while they were there she was preoccupied with them, and when they left she went right back into her state of deep and uninterrupted loneliness. She talked about joining therapy groups and counselling groups. She had even run them for others in recent years. Now everything was so different that her critical judgment of the group process kept her from having any of the usual benefits of the group activity.

When we tried to explore why she was not able to get the benefits of various forms of therapeutic intervention, she admitted that her familiarity with the whole process as a professional seemed to separate her from the benefits she needed as a non-professional, an ordinary lonely person. She was even a little jealous of those who could know the benefits of healing friendships when she with her superior understanding seemed to be denied them.

4

After exploring her feelings of loneliness from many different angles, I said, 'Those of us who work within the psychological disciplines know that all behaviour has meaning. It may sometimes be obscured and difficult to find, but wherever there is effect there is also necessarily a cause. If your loneliness is an effect, what is it the effect of, where does it come from, and why do you feel it is necessary to hold on to it and amplify it?' These questions sent her into a long period of quiet contemplation.

Finally she looked at me and said, 'I guess I have been waiting a long time for somebody to ask me those questions. When you put it like that, I have to approach it from quite a different way.' Then she was quiet again for a long time and I listened to her quietness.

Her response after much thinking was quite simple. 'I think I know. I need this loneliness. I have discovered more about myself and my deep inner being in the last couple of years than I have ever known. My loneliness has been painful but it has been creative. I don't want to give it up for some inner peace that would end my creative self-discovery. My loneliness has been important for me. At least, I am not ready to give it up for whatever its alternative might be.'

We mislead ourselves if we think loneliness is all bad. While it may be anguished at times, it sets to work deep within us those processes that might never stir without the events that precipitate our new needs and our new efforts to satisfy them. Robinson Crusoe would surely have chosen to escape the hazards of shipwreck, but being shipwrecked he found inner resources to create a new and more significant life. Loneliness may be part of a larger process. Never sell your loneliness short until you have assessed what it may be doing for you at the core of your being.

Rachel was a surprise to me. I was driving several hundred miles to an engagement and saw what I assumed was a young lad with a backpack and other gear. I stopped to give him a ride, as I needed company on a long drive. It was not until my passenger began to speak that I realized I had a Rachel rather than a Richard.

Rachel had an interesting story to tell. She was an Israeli. She had lived most of her life on a Kibbutz. She said it was a great way of life and she valued it, but there was always something lacking. Some personal dimension of life seemed to be missing. So she set out to find it.

She had heard much about the United States. She had relatives here. She decided to visit them. But each time she encountered these relatives there was initial warmth and interest, and then it rapidly withered away. She said she didn't know whether it was her fault or theirs, but in short, things went sour. Then she set out again on her quest. New people, new things, new places, but the same old feelings.

As we talked casually about her experience and her feelings, Rachel unfolded a deep loneliness. She said, 'You know, its a strange thing. All my life I've been so aware of being a Jew that I have never had time to become aware of who I am.' As we explored this statement and the feelings that went with it, we confronted an existential form of loneliness that is so much a part of our age. People have been made so aware of the externals of life that they have lost sight of the internal component of being. This has been a part of the value system that emphasizes things and the production of things. The work ethic that would give meaning to life through productivity loses sight of the value of just being.

Recent events in Jewish history have tended to emphasize the need for group solidarity and national productivity. The person may get lost in the process. Rachel was saying that she was afraid she was a lost soul and she desperately needed to find herself. She was lonely for her true nature. So she had set out on her own private pilgrimage to find that part of herself for which she was lonely, the self within that had been largely neglected in her life-experience.

As Rachel talked about her quest for that other part of herself she said some interesting and revealing things. She said, 'I think I am becoming another Wandering Jew, and I will probably never find what I'm looking for because it probably isn't there.' In one pregnant sentence she gave a capsule history of a sensitive people who confronted the burden of consciousness and sought to find its cosmic expression. And it may be that it will never be found out there as something that lives apart, but may rather be found, if at all, in that inner quality of being that is at home in the universe, not because of a tradition but in spite of it.

6

Then Rachel with a little shrug of despair said, 'But you know, I am afraid to stop looking because then life might just fall apart. Now what do you make of that?' It was more important to explore what she would make of it, and we spent many miles trying to see what she meant by this compulsive drive to find meaning for herself. She said she had tried to find herself through sex, but that it was always less fulfilling than she had hoped. She said she had tried to find this other part of her being through education, but that it never seemed to address her problem. She said she was trying to find it in travel and further exploration of the external world, but so far it hadn't helped much. Now she was concerned about finding something that really wasn't there. Was her quest futile and meaningless?

Seldom have I met and explored in depth the meaning of existential loneliness as I did with Rachel. She moved into my life by chance and we traversed many miles together. She was a warm, intelligent and sensitive person. But when we came to the place where we went our separate ways, she said, 'Thanks for the ride and the talk. Wish me luck', and disappeared.

What had Rachel been saying? The inner being struggles to find its meaning in communication and relationship, but there is always unfinished business. There always seems to be more to life than we find. Sometimes we admit defeat and withdraw into unresolved existential loneliness, knowing that it will never really happen. And then sometimes, like Rachel, we set out on our own desperate search for that something else that we know must be there, half fearing that we will never find it, but not daring to stop looking. For many more miles I relived our conversation and thought of the courageous quest of my Wandering Jew. And with all my heart I did wish her luck.

Glenn was a little old cabinet-maker. Most of his fingers had been caught in the power plane at one time or another, and his shortened and stubby fingers seemed inadequate for the delicate work he did with wood. I first met him when I was looking for a hutch. I enjoyed talking with him, for he seemed to enjoy company.

One day he became philosophical and talked about his

many years, for he was eighty-six. I asked, 'When are you going to retire?' His answer came quickly and emphatically, 'Oh, never if I can help it.' Then he went on to tell me what his work meant to him.

'My work's the only thing I've got left. If I give this up I'll be dead in no time. I tried to retire once but it didn't work. That was about ten years ago. Then my wife died and I came over to my shop more and more. It was too lonely around the house. And people came in here and talked. I don't need the money, mind you. I could get along without working. But here I can think and work at the same time. I think working is good for me. Don't you?'

As with many questions, people give their own answers if they are given a little time, so I said: 'Glenn, just how do you mean that?' He laughed a bit and then said, 'Well, you're suppose to know what's good for people, aren't you? I really don't know what I'd do if I didn't have this shop here. I love my machines. We have always worked well together. We seem to fit. They sit here just waiting for me. When we work together things begin to happen. Boards become a table. Trees become chests and hutches. I don't know what there is about it really, but it seems like life to me.'

I didn't say anything, because I didn't want to interrupt so beautiful a soliloquy. He turned around from his work-bench as if to see if I were listening. Then he continued. 'Nobody can know what loneliness is until they have lived with somebody for fifty-six years. It seems like life is finished when they've finished. But life has to go on. You can't just die of loneliness. You have to fight it. So my shop was always a part of my life and I came back to it. I'm going to work 'til I die.'

You can understand why I like to visit Glenn and watch him at work. He is a craftsman who takes plenty of time with his work. He is creating things to enrich life, and as long as he does that he is enriching his own life. He knows the pain of loss and loneliness, but he is fighting it, and you can be sure he will fight it to the end. However, his loneliness is not an enemy, for he has made friends with it and uses it to stimulate his creativeness. He and his shop, he and his machines have a pact with life and they are working well together to keep it.

Sandra called for an appointment. She was a ski instructor on a nearby slope. She merely said that she had a problem that she wanted to talk about.

When Sandra came she was the picture of health and vigour. In addition to being beautiful, she had a glow about her as well as a lithe and athletic build. She walked with assurance and poise, so I was not quite prepared for the explication of the problem that was bothering her.

After a few introductory remarks she asked, 'Did you see *Roots* on that television series?' When I admitted that I had not, she went on, 'Well, I did. And that's my problem. I wish I hadn't, yet I'm glad I did, if you know what I mean. Its just one of those things that happens and you are not quite the same.' She looked at me as if to see whether or not I shared her thoughts, so I responded, 'I think I know what you are driving at, but you had better fill in the details so that I am sure.'

Well, it's a long story, but I will try to keep it as short as possible. I simply don't know who I am. You probably guessed it, I'm adopted. Now you couldn't have had better parents than I have had. They have surrounded my life with love. They have given me the best of everything. They have protected my freedom to be what I want to be. They have never lied to me, I'm sure, but still I don't know who I am. They don't know. That was their agreement with the adoption agency. They would not stop me if I tried to find out. I'm sure of that. But the problem is deeper.

I guess it all started when I was studying nursing. We had a course in physiology, and one day one of the doctors gave a lecture on haemoglobin, the nature of the blood and its parts. It was fascinating, but he kept saying that the blood carries the genetic marks that determine who you are. He talked about genes and chromosomes. But that night I had a frightening dream. I was lost and couldn't find my way out of an endless forest. I'm no psychoanalyst, but I know enough about dreams to know they are trying to tell you something. So I faced it. I didn't know who my real parents were, so I couldn't know myself really. That's kind of frightening, isn't it?

My parents had been so good to me that I couldn't bring

myself to do anything that would embarrass them or make them think I didn't love them or appreciate all they had done for me. I wanted to start my search for my real parents, but I kept putting it off. The uncertainty was killing me, but doing something about it seemed so unreasonable. And then there was *Roots*. It really shook me up. I realized something for the first time that really shattered me. You know I'm married. Swell guy. We got married four years ago. I got pregnant. I convinced myself that I had been exposed to *rubella*, German measles, and had an abortion. Then about a year later I was pregnant again. Careless of me, but I found another good excuse for an abortion. And now for the first time I think I know what was going on. I think I felt I shouldn't bring a child into the world unless I was sure of my ancestry and genetic inheritance. I just can't go on like this. I really would like to be a mother, but I am fighting something awful inside. Do you see what I mean? Can you see what my problem is?

Her story, poured out with intense feeling, had left her rather exhausted, so I took a little time to restate her problem and give her some breathing space. Then I summed up by agreeing that the implications of her feelings of lost identity were so far-reaching that she was wise in confronting them.

She accepted this reassurance and support and went on:

Roots, roots. Where are my roots? It's a terrible thing to be an uprooted human being and not know the most important things you need to know to face yourself and face parenthood. What can I possibly do about it? I've got to do something. I can't go on like this. My whole future is involved. I'm desperate. I don't want to hurt anyone, but look what I've done already. I've got to do something.

Sandra was confronting another form of loneliness that was related to her deep longing to find that part of herself from which she had been separated. She was lonely for her real family, her biological roots, her sense of personal relationship to her own tradition. Whether or not she would or could find it was problematical. Having found it, she might be even more distressed. But the emotional roots of her loneliness were clear. She did not know who she was biologically, and she longed to know in order to face life and its responsibilities.

John had been in a serious road accident. He had many broken bones and several internal injuries. He was taken to a distant medical centre where special surgery and rehabilitation procedures were available. He was so far from home that visits from friends and relatives were few and separated by long stretches of lonely time.

John's life was full and interesting until that moment when serious injury seemed to change everything. Now he was isolated, limited in action, restrained in mobility. For an active, gregarious person these conditions seemed often to be worse than his physical injuries.

One day John's minister, who was attending a conference in the distant city, stopped to see him. He stopped at the nurses' desk to make the initial inquiry. The nurse said, 'Oh, we're so glad you have come. John is not responding. He is doing well physically and everything is being done that can be done, but he is so low in spirits. We can't seem to do anything to shake him out of it. We feel that he is losing the will to live. If there is anything you can do to cheer him up, please; for God's sake do it. We're feeling helpless.

When the pastor approached, John seemed apathetic and listless. He did not seem willing or able to enter into conversation. So the pastor sat quietly by the bed and held his hand. This went on for some time, perhaps fifteen minutes. Then John turned his head a bit and said, 'Did you ever know what it was like to be completely helpless?' To pursue it the pastor asked, 'John, just how do you mean that?'

John went on, 'I can't go to the bathroom. I lie here and let others handle my body, wash me and wipe me. They feed me and do everything for me that I used to do for myself. I am more helpless than a baby. A baby doesn't know what helplessness means. I do. I could manage my life. Now I am a worthless human being. This kind of existence isn't worth living. I'd be better off dead.'

The last statements had a tentative quality about them, as if John were asking for disagreement. But simple reassurance in his condition might be considered rejection of his feelings, so this was avoided. Rather, an effort was made to set the course

11

of thinking and feeling in another direction.

The pastor said, 'John, it must be terrible for you to go through this period of slow and painful healing. But to say that you are helpless seems to ignore something very important. The most important parts of your being are still under your control. Your thinking and feeling processes are yours and they are working well. When you feel lonely and helpless, it is quite natural to be depressed and apprehensive. But that part of your living is still yours to manage. You can think of one thing at a time. You can decide what that will be. When you hurt, your world can be reduced to just you and your hurt. But your mind at work can expand your world. You can make room for more living by the way you think about what is going on. You can help the doctors and nurses or you can frustrate them. Just a while ago one of the nurses expressed her concern. They want so much to help you. You decide whether you will let them or not.'

John's eyes moistened and some tears formed. 'You can't imagine what it's like here week after week. You do feel like giving up. But I do want to help the doctors and nurses. They are great people. I guess I was feeling so sorry for myself that I was forgetting about them. I tried being cheerful for a while, then it seemed to back up on me. It didn't seem to be honest. I can see I was letting things get to me. Maybe I can change my attitude.'

After a while the idea of becoming an active partner with the healing team began to make sense, and John began to see that his attitude could slow up the healing or speed it along as he chose. If he let his loneliness and despair run his life, his behaviour would be self-defeating. But if he actively worked with his friends on the staff, his loneliness would be reduced and life would not only seem better, it would be better. In addition a programme of communication and support was established. Often we forget how lonely those who are sick and hospitalized can be. Loneliness is not a monolithic state of being. It is a two-way street. We can move towards the lonely if we expect them to move towards us.

We have examined several different types of loneliness to see what they look and feel like in the lives of those who experience it.

There was the loneliness of the adolescent and the need for understanding and friendship.

There was the loneliness of the bereaved woman whose skill as a psychologist complicated her own emotional problem.

There was the existential loneliness of the young woman who was searching the world for a lost dimension of her own being.

There was the loneliness of the elderly person who was fighting desperately to keep life meaningful.

There was the loneliness of the adopted woman who sought the missing rootage of her life.

There was the loneliness of the critically ill and injured person separated from the life he had known and reduced to helplessness and despair.

Loneliness comes in many forms, and often it is a disguised emotion. Yet there is something of the Robinson Crusoe in all of us, as we seek to understand our needs for competence in handling whatever form of loneliness moves in upon our lives.

2

Why People Become Lonely

Anyone who has experienced loneliness is apt to be puzzled by it. It hurts so much, and yet it is not a disease. It is painful, but you cannot put your finger on any one spot that hurts. It makes you miserable all over, but it is not like a broken leg. It is not so much a physical condition as it is a response within the external conditioning circumstances. One reason loneliness is so baffling is because we have trouble defining it, and even when we struggle towards a definition we find that the defining of the condition is not an explanation of it.

Often we try to define loneliness by locating it in human experience. We can find loneliness in the nuclear family, the small unit of relation that cramps life and puts stress on those who are bound up in it. It is found in mental illness where normal communication and relationship breaks down. It is found in depression, where persons feel helpless to control life and so withdraw into themselves. Loneliness is often found in the self-judgment that goes along with failure. When a person is told that cancer cells are at work within, there seems to be a separation from all the rest of healthy humanity that causes loneliness. When a person becomes deaf and is embarrassed by asking others to repeat or speak louder, there is a separation from conversation that isolates and causes loneliness. When blindness afflicts a person, there is a breakdown of the usual mode for paying attention to what is going on around one, and this leads to separation, isolation and loneliness.

When a person is endowed with a high IQ, there may be a special form of loneliness, because the mind works more rapidly and makes instant connections which others may be slow in doing, and so there become fewer and fewer persons who understand or want to understand what seems so natural for the highly endowed. Specialization tends to isolate persons, and the field of special interest for the nuclear physicist or the molecular biologist centres on language and concepts so unusual that only a small group of people can share the language or the interest. Moral consciousness that tends to pass judgment on social processes that are generally accepted may produce the type of loneliness that the pacifist feels during wartime or the temperance advocate feels during the round of Christmas parties.

The inner climate of a person may cause separation from others, and the creative spirit of the artist may be bought at the price of a discipline that isolates and causes loneliness. Deeply planted emotional states that we call moods may make it difficult for a person to relate to others, with resultant loneliness. Fear of failure or fear of ridicule, or the fear of what others may think, may drive persons away from social contact and isolate the fearful person in a special type of loneliness. Feelings of insecurity may so overwhelm life that a person retreats from an adventure that seems threatening and so gets caught in one of life's lonely eddies. On the other hand, there is the loneliness of the pioneer who moves ahead of the crowd or his times and is out there where companionship is sacrificed for the pioneering spirit. Often the person of courage, making stands for unpopular or hazardous ideas or actions, is separated from the crowd and suffers loneliness. The idealist who refuses to compromise may pay the price in loneliness.

Sometimes human sexuality causes loneliness, when the unattractive whose needs may be great are ignored. The unwanted and rejected child can have an overwhelming form of loneliness that comes with emotional abandonment and all of life may be marred by it. The elderly whose main relationship is the television, with its one-way input into life, may lose the ability to respond. The stranger in a community, a school or a job may have a special type of loneliness when everyone else seems to be known and the stranger cannot share this easy and comfortable relationship.

So we see that there are many ways of experiencing loneliness. Each of us can recall the times and experiences of loneliness, and can identify with some illustration that comes from the last few paragraphs. We may be able to move back into one or more of these times of loneliness to try to recall

15

the feelings we had that made us hurt so much, deep inside.

What feelings were involved? When did they come over us? Can we recall anything about the feelings?

Feelings have their own integrity. They are an important part of life, but they cannot be measured by the usual standards of measurement. We cannot buy a yard of comfort, a quart of hope or a pound of sympathy. All of these feelings and their negative counterparts are usually felt beyond the power of reason or the use of thinking. Sometimes it seems that thought and feeling are as hard to mix as oil and water.

Feelings also have their own individuality. We cannot feel anybody else's feelings. We can recognize their right to have their feelings, but they are as personal as breathing or seeing. When we are lonely we are using a set of feelings that are very much our own. In fact, part of the problem is that they are so much our own that we have difficulty in sharing them. We feel isolated by the feelings we have.

Perhaps the best way to isolate some of the components of lonely feelings is to illustrate them. Let us take three common experiences of loneliness and try to isolate the feelings that were active in each case.

You are a child. You are in school. There is a special programme for a special celebration. You are assigned a part and work hard to learn the words you are to say. All seems to be going well until that moment when the teacher gives you a gentle nudge and you find yourself walking out on stage. But this is different. This is not like the times of practising the lines or looking forward to the event. It is dark, and you see many eyes reflected back at you. These are not the classmates you know, but big people. You are overcome with strange feelings. You begin to twist and turn. You hear people sniggering and this makes it worse. Your mind goes blank and you can't remember the first line. The teacher whispers it to you and you repeat it, and then cannot remember the second line. Futile efforts follow, and the serious efforts quickly move to cruel humour and then on to personal tragedy as tears come and the teacher rescues you and leads you off to painful defeat and humiliating failure.

What were the feelings during this brief episode? There was anticipation, preparation and then strangeness and the unexpected. Then there was paralysing anxiety that shut off

16

the mind from its expected action. Then the anxiety was compounded by laughter which directed attention away from the assignment and towards the embarrassed self. The teacher's effort to start your mind working again failed because so much attention was centred on your feelings that little was left for anything else. So the teacher rescues you from more ridicule and you retreat with feelings of pain and failure. You discover what a lonely feeling it can be to be out in front all by yourself. The impact of the experience emotionally may be so great that you say to yourself, 'Never again'. So you may have great difficulty in ever moving towards any public appearance. You may become shy and retreat from any group of people that seem to be looking at you. You may avoid getting into situations where many people are present, and social life may be severely injured for years to come because of one event that was an emotional catastrophe.

A second episode, and you are a teenager. You feel that you are deeply in love. The daydreams and fantasies swirl through your thoughts. The object of your love has heroic qualities and is constantly demonstrating them, though always indirectly, because you have never said more than a casual greeting to each other. Every act and attitude is charged with the emotion that is directed towards the object of your love. But there is no return. Thoughts of sacrifice and noble love unrequited constantly race through your thought. Then there is the day when you become sure that the object of your love really loves another. There is despair and anguish. There are thoughts of self-destruction and the cruelty of life. You want to retreat into the painful loneliness and take vows in a religious order, for there can never be a love like that you have known.

The emerging ego of the adolescent is a strange mixture of toughness and fragility. Tough in the sense that most of us survive this stressful period in life, and fragile in that we can go through periods of rapid change and unstable emotions that show our insecurity and uncertainty. There can be feelings of despair along with romantic idealism. There can be times when bravado covers our tenderness. The need for social acceptance and approval is important during this time, for there is an effort to grow beyond the safety of the family into the security of the larger social group. Because of the vulnerability of this period there is great possibility for injury and rejection. So many of us during this time of life first experience deep periods of feeling lost, separated and alone. We try to break through the barriers of our isolation with drugs and cosmetics, flaunting our assets and skills, yet none of these things may be able to break through the tentative and protective wall we build around ourselves to protect the fragile and emerging sense of who we are. The forward movement of life usually carries us along into greater maturity, but the scars that may be left on life during this period can be deep and have a lasting effect on our relations with others and the inner climate of insecurity that breeds loneliness within ourselves.

Third, you are an adult. You have emerged as a person with social competence, economic security and basic good health. You feel confident within yourself that life is going well. You are married and have a family. Then you are obliged for business reasons to move to another city in quite a different part of the country. At first the chores of moving occupy time and attention. But the efforts to establish roots in a new community seem to be constantly thwarted. At church the theology, emotional climate and mixture of superstition and prejudice against ideas quite basic to your life cause uneasiness. In business a close-knit 'in' group conspires to exclude new persons and ideas. In social life an unfamiliar political and personal set of attitudes makes relationships difficult or impossible. It seems impossible at every point to establish any meaningful human relations. Then illnesses begin to develop, suspiciously like psychogenic messages. Irritability increases within the family and a variety of stress-points in life begin to emerge. No one seems to be able to put a finger on the cause of the changes, but all agree that everything seems to have gone wrong after the move. When life is pulled up by the roots and the old, familiar and life-sustaining patterns are lost, loneliness creeps slowly in, touching all of the support systems that have been taken for granted and are not missed until they are gone.

What has been happening emotionally? What have been the feelings that resulted from the uprooting experience? Uprootedness in life is one of the major causes of the painful feelings of isolation, separation and dislocation. When Alvin Toffler wrote about 'future shock', he was talking in part about the impact of threatening mobility in our culture where on the average every family moves once in four years. Pulling a family up by the roots affects the sustaining structure of life. More than we realize, the familiar patterns of our thinking and feelings are built and sustained by group forces and social life. We move into these structuring patterns gradually and they become a part of our existence. When circumstance disrupts the functioning of this sustaining structure, life seems to fall apart. The emotions that are incident to this falling apart are not easily identified, for they tend to be generalized. But we can discover them if we try.

Deeply rooted in our being is an apprehension that manifests itself when we confront the different, the strange and the unfamiliar. We may sense it when we travel. We look forward to visiting another country and a different culture. But we notice that the new and different, or the old and strange, begin to make us uneasy. After a few weeks we hear ourselves saying, 'This has been interesting, but it will be nice to be home.' The longing for the familiar asserts itself with greater insistence, and when finally we get close to home and the familiar places, we express relief and are apt to comment, 'No matter where we go, this is the best place of all.' In effect, we have been saying that something deep within us was out of adjustment to different things and strange people and languages, and we are comfortable when we return to the patterns of life where adjustment is at a minimum and we can relax in the familiar.

In the stressful adjustments that a family must make to its uprootedness, we sense that multiple adaptations are taking place all at once. The stresses that occur are amplified because we cannot find balance and stability with others who are making similar adjustments. Things tend to fall apart and jangled emotions show through.

As we try to isolate some of the feelings that are a part of the hurt of loneliness we find that they come in three different forms. There are the painful feelings that are part of a developmental process and show up in the illustrations of childhood and adolescence. Then there are the circumstantial causes of loneliness that may come with uprootedness and confronting the new and strange. And another set of emotions that cause loneliness may be found in something deep within human nature and the need for relationship that is constantly unfulfilled, and this we would call the existential rootage of loneliness. Let us look at these varied components of loneliness more closely, for this may help us understand why it hurts so much.

Children live completely in the world of feelings. In the early stages they are so helpless and dependent that their sensitivity to others is great. Nothing is so shattering to a child as to feel abandoned, left alone. Children cry out in their distress because there is such a clear tie between their distressed feelings and those other concerned persons about them who can relieve their distress. Because a child has no sense of time or space, even a short period of time seems endless, and the impatience of the child is based on the sense of immediacy that pervades all of life. The child can become quite insecure when the mother is out of sight for even a short time.

We have all seen a lost child in a large store. The mother may be at the next counter, but when the child loses sight of the mother there is frenzied searching about, and then crying that affirms pain at the feelings of being lost or abandoned. When dependency is great, the fears of separation are life-threatening, and a painful emotion is generated which Colin Parkes calls 'separation anxiety'. The child is not able to be objective and reason things out. The child does not say, 'My mother does not act like the person who would deliberately abandon me, so I will wait quietly here, for I know she will soon find me.' The rational aspects of the behaviour precludes that type of careful consideration of all the facts.

Most neurotic behaviour has a quality of the non-rational about it. Neurotic behaviour seems to involve a retreat to childish forms of behaviour. The frenzied activity of the person who feels abandoned carries some of the early emotions of childhood, and this component of loneliness can trigger powerful recollection of early fears. Certainly some of the pain of loneliness we may feel in adulthood is an echo of the early childhood fears of loss or abandonment.

Another period of emotional stress comes with the adjustment years when we are part-child and part-adult. We make tentative moves out into the world of adult relationships and responsibilities, but then want to be able to retreat into the security of childhood when the going gets tough. But often this retreat is not possible, and we face hostility and rejection without protection and this can be painful.

Often the initial exploration of this in-between stage of life is found in game-playing or sports. Here the competition and the opportunity to win and lose gives us some practice in ego-strengthening behaviour. Along with the game-playing there are bumps, bruises and conflict. We learn to accept some of the injury because we feel it is a part of something greater. Teamwork towards a common goal of victory provides support and strength. Even in failure and defeat we are not alone. This experimental game-playing of adolescence may have to do with sports, love or ideals for living. But it is important because it is basic to the development of our inner skills for living.

This is not always an easy period of life to grow through because we may be faced with circumstances we cannot control. In her autobiography, Margaret Mead tells of the experience in her youth when she went off to DePauw University, filled with hope and excitement. She wanted to share campus life to the full. This included the social life of a sorority. But she was rejected, and the wounds of that rejection cut deeply into her being. She survived the loss, but its effect was so great that it made her sensitive to the needs of excluded people all the rest of her life. The loneliness that comes with this form of rejection may be so damaging to college freshmen that they never quite get over it. Their first venture out into a world where they are measured on their own merits alone may damage a fragile ego severely, or it may hasten the development of inner strength that makes a person better able to deal with the hard knocks of life. What makes the difference will be a major consideration for us as we move on into this exploration of separation traumas and loneliness.

Because the ego is apt to be tender during adolescence, it is possible for emotional damage to interrupt development at this point. Then we get the type of person who becomes the perpetual adolescent. They want to play games all of their lives, hoping that eventually they can become a winner. They may move from one game to another, trying to find one that suits their emotional needs. In the process they tend to put off the tasks of achieving true maturity. When it is confined to sports it may not be so bad, but when they make an unending game of love they make tentative what should be a sustaining commitment, and life suffers in the consequence.

Many of the roots of loneliness can be found in the developmental processes of our living. But there are also many aspects of the circumstantial events of life that can cause loneliness. Often these are the things that we cannot control. Once I served as a counsellor in a military replacement centre. Here the maladjusted were sent back for reassignment. In exploring the causes of their inability to adapt to the exigencies of military life I often found that loneliness was a major component of their problem. The separation from all they had known in their past, and the new and unfamiliar life-style, was more than they could adjust to. They were uncomfortable with a new type of discipline. They disagreed with the new value system. They were distressed by their forced associations. In the past they chose their associates carefully, and now they were thrust into intimate living conditions with people they would never have associated with before. The constant stress of this type of life became intolerable, and they broke down under the pressure and were sent back for rehabilitation and reassignment.

These circumstantial factors producing the distress of loneliness are so numerous that I cannot begin to explore them all, but I can give illustrations. For instance, the basic endowment of a person may tend to cause isolation. A mentally retarded child may not understand why he is repeatedly 'left behind' or separated from the other children he has known, to be put with strangers again and again. It may also be true at the other end of the intelligence scale, for the exceptionally well-endowed child will have difficulty understanding why everyone else seems so slow to understand. In order to maintain a social relationship, the bright child may play at being stupid in order to have others laugh with him and feel acceptance.

Learning difficulties may cause isolation. Family tensions may produce loneliness. Geographical conditions may compound personal problems. The child bussed into school from an outlying farm may have difficulty establishing social patterns in school because catching the bus back home may interfere with the extra-curricular activities that are so much a part of the educational community. Various forms of physical impairment tend to isolate and produce loneliness. This may be related to hearing loss, visual limitation or chronic illnesses. It becomes doubly difficult for a person to experience normal development when these extra problems have to be dealt with.

Of course, mobility and moving from one community to another causes loneliness. The child of migrant workers suffers from interrupted education, severed friendships and conditions that lead to social maladaptation. The family of the rapidly advancing young executive may have many of the emotional problems of the child of migrant parents. The place in the social structure may be different, but the stresses and the needs for adaptive skills may be comparable.

Even the persons who have special privileges may experience deprivation and isolation. The youth who has had everything provided all through childhood may be in a more precarious condition than the child who has had to learn to cope with deprivation. Skills in learning to get along without everything desired may be important for learning to live. The drug problems of the privileged youths may be related to the weakness of ego-strength caused by the lack of experience in dealing creatively with life stresses, so chemical agents are used to get away from it all. This, then, is a form of circumstantial loneliness.

Harvey Cox has pointed out the types of loneliness and separation that can arise from being too close to other people. The tendency to make people into non-people can be observed in a crowded subway or large apartment houses. Being too close to people can limit freedom and cause a special threat to being. Experiments with mice showed that overcrowding was life-destroying. When too many mice were confined to a small area, many died of what appeared to be stress-related diseases, and others became confused and had role disturbance, homosexual activity and a marked decrease in births. We may be seeing comparable responses at the human level.

When we consider that the greatest migration in human

history has taken place in this century, we can sense the dislocation and loneliness that has gone with it. In the year 1900 more than seventy per cent of all persons in my country lived on farms or in rural communities. By 1975 just the opposite was true. This rapid migration from the places where people knew each other and local customs to the unfamiliar and stressful ways of city living could not help but produce separation anxiety and various forms of retreat towards imagined areas of security which were not secure at all, as they were movement away from people when what was needed was more valid forms of relationship.

We have all been involved in circumstantial forms of loneliness-producing life experiences. Some of them have helped us grow in strength and adaptability. Others have been hard to manage and produce long lasting scars on life.

In addition to developmental and circumstantial causes of painful loneliness, there is also the basic impact of something deep within our own natures that is constantly at work. A South Dakota Indian said, 'The sun comes up each day; the wind stirs the trees; the great spirit moves throughout the land and we meet him – alone.' A modern psychologist writes, 'We become lonely because it is our nature to be lonely when our lives are without certain significant relationships, just as it is our nature to react to other deficit situations with hunger or with chill.'[1]

When we are hungry, stomach muscles contract with a special form of pain. When we are cold, our bodies try to adapt to the change and we are chilled or feel the pain of frostbite. When our sensitive consciousness is placed under stress, our spirits become starved or frostbitten and yet another form of distress assails us. Where does existential loneliness come from?

Each human being is endowed with a special form of sensitivity that we call consciousness. As far as we know it is not found in its human form anywhere else in nature. The ancients thought it was that portion that was made in the image of God. Jesus saw his mission as that of helping people develop this inner kingdom so that the relation between the God-conscious individual and the God of which he was conscious could be brought to its most abundant form of development.

This endowment of consciousness is both a great privilege and an unbearable burden. It gives life special opportunities for awareness and demands of life a discipline and responsibility that we would often rather avoid. It makes it possible for us to be self-conscious, socially conscious and cosmically conscious. We want to be at home within ourselves, in our relationships with others and with the cosmic dimensions of being. But this is an enormous task. It calls for all our skills and our heightened awareness. It calls for self-acceptance, socially conscious attitudes and behaviour, and an undergirding faith that makes it possible for us to be at home in the universe.

This is a burdensome task for several reasons. We are seldom completely at peace with ourselves because we have different urges and goals, and they vary from time to time, so inconsistency comes into life. We want to be secure in our relations with others, but do not want to assume the discipline that guarantees constant reciprocity. We do not want to forgive as we are forgiven, have mercy as we hope for mercy, and love with the unselfishness that we would like to have shown us.

So our capacity for consciousness makes it difficult to communicate and relate. If we cannot understand ourselves, how can we expect anyone else to understand us? If we do not love God with heart, and soul and mind and strength, how can we hope to feel secure in a cosmic presence? We often feel trapped within our own deeper needs. We want to be completely understood, but we do not know how. We want to be able to know as we are known, but we fall short. Language can never carry all the meaning we would want, because at best it is a structure of symbols and not the real thing. So we are never able to express all our feelings and find all the security our spirits desire. So there is always an existential residue of unrequited need, and we feel strangers in a universe unaware or unconcerned. We try to invest what is beyond self with meaning enough to reciprocate our needs, but it seldom proves satisfactory, and deep loneliness pervades our humanity. In fact what is called the human predicament is largely made up of this deeply-rooted feeling of inadequacy or incompleteness. Therein lies some of the loneliness that is most difficult to resolve.

I have tried to show why loneliness hurts so much. We have seen it as a cluster of emotions that have their roots deep in life. We have seen that there are many ways in which loneliness can be experienced. I have tried to illustrate it in various phases of life and in different human experiences.

In the first chapter we tried to see how loneliness looks in contemporary life and experience. Then we looked at various classic examples of catastrophic separation. I have tried to assess the emotions that are a part of the painful experience of loneliness to see where the feelings come from. I have broken up the nature of loneliness into three major components, the developmental, the circumstantial and the existential. Now that we have illustrated and explored the way the emotion feels when we encounter it, we are better prepared to look more closely at a classic story about loneliness, and see how Robinson Crusoe developed skills in coping with his isolation and loneliness.

3

Robinson Crusoe Up to Date

I was recently speaking to a conference of members of government agencies working with isolated and lonely people. I asked how many of those present had read the classic novel *Robinson Crusoe*, by Daniel Defoe. About ninety per cent raised their hands. Then I asked how many had read the book in childhood. About the same number of hands were raised. I thought to myself how unfortunate it was that most people read this book before they are able to understand or appreciate it.

Undoubtedly *Robinson Crusoe* is one of the first in-depth studies of human loneliness. It may well be that it is also a source of insight into one of our major contemporary problems. So let us look behind the adventure story that is so intriguing in childhood to see what it tells us about that painful experience of isolation, loneliness and inner pain that seems to afflict so many people today. Let us see what it can tell us about the nature of loneliness and the ways of managing it. Skipping the early adventures of running away from home, storms at sea, enslavement in Africa and a period as plantation owner in South America, we come to the part of the story that tells about the shipwreck and his struggle to survive in the heavy seas. Then he alone of all those aboard lands safely on a beach which he later found was part of an island, completely deserted except for animal life and birds.

> I was now landed and safe on shore, and began to look up and thank God that my life was saved in a case wherein there was some minutes before scarce any room to hope. I believe it is impossible to express to the life what the ecstasies and transports of the soul are, when it is so saved, as I may say, out of the very grave (p.36).[1]

So was recorded the first feeling with deliverance from shipwreck and the sea.

27

But such emotions may change like quicksilver. And a few paragraphs after these words of ecstasy we come upon the changed mood.

After I had solaced my mind with the comfortable part of my condition, I began to look round me to see what kind of place I was in, and what was next to be done, and I soon found my comforts abate, and that in a word I had a dreadful deliverance; for I was wet, had no clothes to shift me, nor any thing either to eat or drink to comfort me, neither did I see any prospect before me, but that of perishing with hunger, of being devoured by wild beasts; and that which was particularly afflicting to me was that I had no weapon either to hunt and kill any creature for my sustenance, or to defend myself against any other creature that might desire to kill me for theirs (p.36).

After spending a night in a tree as a simple device of security, Crusoe assessed his condition the next day and was filled with grief because of the familiar 'if only'. As he put it,

A little after noon I found the sea very calm, and the tide ebbed so far out that I could come within a quarter mile of the ship; and here I found a fresh renewing of my grief, for I saw evidently, that if we had kept on board, we had all been safe, that is to say, we had all got safe on shore, and I had not been so miserable as to be left entirely destitute of all company and comfort, as I was now; this forced tears from my eyes again (p.37).

After retrieving any necessary items from the ship he tried to get them to shore on a hastily made raft. The possibility of another misfortune due to the tide reflected the fragile state of his emotions for he reports:

But here I had like to have suffered a second shipwreck, which, if I had, I think verily would have broke my heart (p.39).

His uncertain emotional state made Crusoe subject to unreasonable and unnecessary fears. As he admits,

I was afraid to lie down on the ground, not knowing but some wild beast might devour me, tho', as I afterwards found, there was really no need for those fears (p.41).

28

The dividing line between wise providence and fearful apprehension for the future becomes obscured by the lonely state. Making secure his first load of provisions, Crusoe set out again for the ship to retrieve as much as he could of those things that might help to sustain his precarious life. He hesitated to leave what he had, for fear it might be raided in his absence. But he overcame one fear in order to protect himself against another. A second raftload from the ship brought all the men's clothes he could find plus canvas from sails and bedding. When he returned he found nothing ashore had been touched but a new dilemma faced him.

A conflict between his needs for security and his needs for companionship presented itself. Should he kill an intruder or try to make friends? Let's look at his choice as he records it.

When I came back, I found no sign of any visitor, only there sat a creature like a wild cat upon one of the chests, which when I came towards it, ran away a little distance, and then stood still; she sat very composed and unconcerned, and looked full in my face, as if she had a mind to be acquainted with me. I presented my gun at her, but as she did not understand it, she was perfectly unconcerned at it, nor did she offer to stir away; upon which I tossed her a bit of bisket, tho' by the way I was not very free of it, for my store was not great. However, I spared her a bit, I say, and she went to it, smelled of it, and ate it, and looked (as pleased) for more (p.42).

His lonely state immediately affected a change in the values he was forced to live by. On another trip to the wrecked ship he reports on his finds and the way he felt about them. On finding a cache of money he reacts so,

I found about thirty six pounds' value in money, some European coin, some Brazil, some pieces of eight, some gold, some silver. I smiled to myself at the sight of this money. 'O drug,' said I aloud, 'what art thou good for? Thou art not worth to me, no, not the taking off of the ground; one of these knives is worth all this heap; I have no manner of use for thee, e'en remain where thou art, and go to the bottom as a creature whose life is not worth saving' (p.43).

Having retrieved all that he could from the ship, he was surprised one morning after a storm to look out and find that the ship was gone. It had broken up in the night, and its remnants had apparently been carried out to sea. A tie with the past was severed and he was now faced with a new and difficult task. This he set about with determination and ordered thinking.

'My thoughts were now wholly employed about securing my self against either savages, if any should appear, or wild beasts, if any were on the island; and I had many thoughts of the method how to do this, and what kind of dwelling to make, whether I should make me a cave in the earth, or a tent upon the earth; and, in short, I resolved upon both, the manner and description of which it may not be improper to give an account of (p.44).

After carefully exploring his situation he set up a list of basic needs. It is interesting to see how his fears and his reason combined to assess his needs. As he puts it,

I consulted several things in my situation which I found would be proper for me: 1st, health and fresh water I just now mentioned; 2ndly, shelter from the heat of the sun; 3rdly, security from ravenous creatures, whether men or beasts; 4thly, a view to the sea, that if God sent any ship in sight, I might not lose any advantage for my deliverance, of which I was not willing to banish all my expectations yet (p.44).

Crusoe set his needs in order. First were the constant needs of existence such as his water supply. Then came his security from the constant impact of the elements. After that followed the possibilities of enemies that might assault his body from without, and finally his nurturing of hope. Often those placed in a precarious position by a newly imposed loneliness find that they think first of food and drink, then of a place to live, and after that some measures for security and then finally some hope for future deliverance or a change that can set them free from their loneliness.

At great effort he built himself what was an almost impregnable fortress, so that he could feel secure and sleep in peace. Sleeping seemed so important to him that it became a major consideration in his security system. Later he had to admit that all of his precautions were unnecessary, for there were no human or animal threats to his security on his island domain. Imagination always seems to get a head start in its focus on the hazards of life.

Once safe and secure, however, he began to have the time to assess his feelings and face the conditions of his life. A new set of concerns moved into the centre of his consciousness. He records them as follows.

And now being to enter into a melancholy relation to a scene of silent life, such perhaps as was never heard of in the world before, I shall take it from its beginning, and continue it in its order. It was, by my account, the 30th of September when I first set foot up on this horrid island, when the sun being, to us, in its autumnal equinox, was almost just over my head, for I reckoned my self, by observation, to be in the latitude of 9 degrees and 22 minutes north of the line (p.48).

One of the first acts of his free time was to try to make sure he knew where he was in relation to all of the rest of mankind.

Not only did he want to be oriented in space and know where he was, he also wanted to be oriented in time and know where he was in relation to the sequence of events in the rest of creation.

After I had been there about ten or twelve days, it came into my thoughts that I should lose my reckoning of time for want of books and pen and ink, and should even forget the Sabbath days from the working days; but to prevent this I cut it with my knife upon a large post, in capital letters, and making it with a great cross I set it up on the shore where I first landed, viz. 'I came on shore here on the 30th of Sept. 1659.' Upon the sides of this square post I cut every day a notch with my knife, and every seventh notch was as long again as the rest, and every first day of the month as long again as that long one, and thus I kept my kalender, my weekly, monthly, and yearly reckoning of time (p.48).

In his struggle for symbols of security in an insecure state he found that knowing where he was in space and time was a point of relationship to the life he had known and with which he wanted to maintain a continuing relationship.

In his isolated state he sought any forms of companionship that would nourish his humanity. He records those symbols of relationship that became especially important to him. These were treasures that had no practical use but apparently had a great personal use. He treasured,

> in particular, pens, ink, and paper, several parcels in the captain's, mate's, gunner's and carpenter's keeping, three or four compasses, some mathematical instruments, dials, perspectives, charts, and books of navigation, all which I huddled together, whether I might want them or no (p.49).

Here was the material for a journal which he faithfully kept. It was a form of communication with himself where he was able to be more objective about himself and his condition. And the navigation instruments made it possible for him to affirm his location in relation to the rest of the world from which he had been so precipitously separated.

A rediscovery of the comforts of religion came to Crusoe as he contemplated his fate.

> I found three very good Bibles which came to me in my cargo from England, and which I had packed up among my things (p.49).

Some of the Psalms were read over and over again as a source of comfort and strength. He began to develop an idea of Providence.

> I had hitherto acted upon no religious foundation at all, indeed, I had very few notions of religion in my head, or had entertained any sense of anything that had befallen me, otherwise than by chance, or, as we lightly say, what pleases God; without so much as enquiring into the end or Providence in these things, or His order in governing events in the world (p.59).
>
> . . . I took up the Bible and began to read . . . the first words that occurred to me were these, 'Call on me in the day of trouble, and I will deliver, and thou shalt glorify me'. . . before I lay down, I did what I had never done in all my life, I kneeled down and prayed to God to fulfil the

promise to me, that if I called upon Him in the day of trouble, he would deliver me; after my broken and imperfect prayer, . . . I fell into a sound sleep (p.70).

In his illness and distress, he sought a cosmic friendship that could mitigate his isolation and loneliness.

Crusoe found that the processes of reason might also be helpful to him in coping with his plight.

I now began to consider seriously my condition, and the circumstance I was reduced to, and I drew up the state of my affairs in writing, not so much to leave them to any that were to come after me, for I was like to have but few heirs, as to deliver my thoughts from daily poring upon them, and afflicting my mind; and as my reason began now to master my despondency, I began to comfort my self as well as I could, and to set the good against the evil, that I might have something to distinguish my case from worse, and I stated it very impartially, like debtor and creditor, the comforts I enjoyed against the miseries I suffered. (p.50).

The processes of reason tend to restore a corrective balance and keep reality in clear focus. In the most distressing circumstances, perspective is essential. When it is lost there is confusion and added distress. When it is regained there is a measure of release from despair. At the end of the process of drawing up his lengthy balance sheet on his life, he concluded,

Upon the whole, here was an undoubted testimony, that there was scarce any condition in the world so miserable, but there was something negative or something positive to be thankful for in it; and let this stand as a direction from the experience of the most miserable of all conditions in this world, that we may always find in it something to comfort our selves from, and to set in the direction of good and evil, on the credit side of the account (p.50).

As soon as reason began to reassert its control over life, Crusoe moved towards therapeutic action. Many troubled spirits have found that they could grow in understanding of themselves and their plight if they could put it into another form of communication. So the diary or the journal makes it possible to talk to oneself in more careful and objective language. Instead of crying out in despair and submerging the self in pity, the journal becomes an instrument for exploring thought and feeling with more care and perspective.

In his journal Robinson expressed his deep feelings and so purged his soul. For months on end, each day was chronicled for its feelings and its insights. Thus there began to emerge a feeling of progressive movement. Not only could he go back and read the record of his days, but he could also project himself into the future with more certainty. The crisis of the journal came when he ran out of ink and was no longer able to record his thoughts and feelings. He tried to invent some writing fluid, but failed. However, the journal had already served its purpose and reasonable ways of talking with himself helped to put life back into balance and perspective.

Another way of assessing what is going on deep within the soul is to translate the metaphor of dreams. In his journal he records, 'I had this terrible dream.' In the dream he saw a powerful flaming figure descend from the heavens with a jolt upon the earth like an earthquake. The figure approached him with a long spear as to kill him. As the weapon was raised the voice said, 'Seeing all these things have not brought thee to repentance, now thou shalt die' (p.65). When he awoke from the dream, he was in a state of panic. His fears and his harrowing adventures had been churning up the lower levels of consciousness, and he was translating them into self-judgment. He was arriving at the place where his plight seemed to be best accounted for as a type of cosmic judgment against him for the failure to establish right relationships between the inner self and the beyond self.

In response to this nightmare he was filled with remorse and tried the ancient method of trying to establish relationship with God through prayer. He cried out in his anguish. His feeble first efforts at prayer mixed his thankfulness at survival with his inner apprehension at the uncertain state of his soul.

Lord! what a miserable creature am I? If I should be sick, I shall certainly die for want of help, and what will become of me! Then the tears burst out of my eyes, and I could say no more for a good while' (p.68).

But the changed state of his inner being was not idle. It was then that he began to remember the advice of his father and the religious training of childhood. The things he discounted and avoided then now became important for the reconstructing of a philosophy of life valid for his troubled state.

The inner struggle for a rational and valid way of looking at life was not easy. In modern perspectives we would say that psychogenic reactions set in. The turbulance of his emotions affected his body functions and he became ill. For days he languished with pain and fevers and from his journal account it would seem that he nearly died. But when he slowly recovered he found a new state of inner peace. His life had been spared. He had confronted death and was not destroyed by it. Now he was set free to live a new life, better grounded in faith in himself, a sense of being more at home in his little universe, and a feeling that God was his friend and not his enemy.

To use his own words to describe the change within he wrote,

My condition began now to be, tho' not less miserable as to my way of living, yet much easier to my mind; and my thoughts being directed, by a constant reading the scripture and praying to God, to things of a higher nature, I had a great deal of comfort within, which till now I knew nothing of; also, as my health and strength returned, I bestirred my self to furnish my self with every thing that I wanted, and make my way of life as regular as I could (p.72).

There was no change in his external state, but something within was changed so that he had new motivation, new willingness to accept and adapt, and an underlying peace that accompanied the change in his perspective on life.

What had been a prison or place of exile changed with his change. He became a lord of the manor, rightfully owning all he surveyed.

I surveyed my kingdom with a secret kind of pleasure . . . to think that this was all my own, that I was king and lord of all this country indefeasibly, and had a right to possession; and if I could convey it, I might have it in inheritance as completely as any lord of a manor in England (p.74).

As is so often the occasion, anniversaries as special days of reckoning release accumulated emotions. On the first anniversary the events of the year poured out in the expression of modified relationships that had come over his life. How did he keep this day? He put together in symbolic form the meaning of his personal pilgrimage from despair to a new inner strength.

I kept this day as a solemn fast, setting it apart to religious exercise, prostrating my self on the ground with the serious humiliation, confessing my sins to God, acknowledging His righteous judgments upon me, and praying to Him to have mercy on me, through Jesus Christ; and having not tasted the least refreshment for twelve hours, even till the going down of the sun, I then eat a bisket cake and a bunch of grapes, and went to bed, finishing the day as I began it' (p.77).

This changed mood made it possible for him to write,

I acquiesced in the dispositions of Providence, which I began now to own and to believe ordered every thing for the best; I say, I quieted my mind with this, and left afflicting my self with fruitless wishes (pp.80f).

The quest for human association persisted. He caught and trained a parrot so that he could have at least some minimal conversation. His dog and cats were able to respond to his words and actions and he invested them with qualities of being, akin to the human.

But then there came the day when he found the print of a human foot upon the beach. He knew he was not alone. With extra precaution he prepared himself for an encounter which might be friendly or unfriendly. Always he had lived as if the moment of encounter would come. The climate was warm and he need wear no clothes, but he wrote that he could never bring himself to this state of nakedness, for even in his loneliness he was aware of social relationships and the proprieties that accompanied them.

But the footprint on the beach had profound impact on his

living. He was alerted to new possibilities, and when the day came for him to rescue the person he named Friday, he was prepared. The humanization and socializing of the island stimulated all Robinson's latent humanity and the desert island became a community. At first, sensible to the problems of society he was afraid lest he be betrayed and face conflict. But this proved to be unwarranted, for of Friday he said,

> Never man had a more faithful, loving, sincere servant, than Friday was to me; without passions, sullenness, or designs, perfectly obliged and engaged; his very affections were tyed to me, like those of a child to a father (p.152).

So life became more secure and more fulfilled as language developed, and companionship was realized.

The varied adventures that marked the end of the story with battles against savages, final rescue and return to homeland seem anti-climactic from our point of view. The theme of release and restoration comes too close to the old idea of 'living happily ever after'. The important parts of the story for our purpose are found in the honest facing of an experience that seems to have a universal quality, the loneliness that touches so much of life.

With an amazing clarity of emotional perception the story takes us through the processes of despair, fear, anxiety and self-rejection to the emergence of a new strength that fights for control, reason, perspective and a faith that is adequate to meet all there is of life, its pain and delight, its loneliness and fractured relationships as well as its joy and supporting relationships.

Robinson Crusoe can open up for us an exploration of one of the more distressing of life's conditions, the awareness of separation from life's sustaining people and values. We can start with the idea that if Robinson Crusoe could find a good life on a deserted and lonely island, it may be possible for us even in the worst of conditions that produce loneliness to find a way out. So let us address ourselves to this task. Thank you, Robinson Crusoe for your help. But now we are on our own.

4

The Social Relationships that Cause Loneliness

Loneliness is based on relationship. So there is always a social context for loneliness. The relationship must exist before it can be broken. Robinson Crusoe had to have roots in civilization before he could experience the acute deprivation he felt on his lonely island. So it is essential for us to understand the meaning of the relationships that characterize the social being before we can find ways to relieve the pain of loneliness when the social ties are disrupted.

When we say a human being is a social creature we are implying far more than the words seem to say. Birth is a social event, for no one is born alone. But before the birth there is some form of social relationship between those who are the parents of the newborn. These parents carry qualities that are passed on from the third and fourth generation, and much, much more.

Recent genetic studies compel us to assume that in each of us there are hundreds of thousands and probably millions of years of long, slow modification and adaptation to life and its demands. All study of the processes of becoming define in one way or another the ways in which social, environmental, chemical and biological forces are at work to provide an amazing endowment for each human being. The social structure into which we are born is a continuation of a historical process that provides us with some major common capacities like the ability to walk upright and to learn a language. Noam Chomsky even posits some mystical process implicit to the brain development and muscular facility that is basic to speech. But similarly the uniqueness of the process of individualization guarantees that there may also be major differences in endowment, mentally and emotionally. These differences may be observed in national, ethnic and cultural traditions. So we observe that most professional basketball players are tall blacks and most jockeys are small-sized whites. Even certain diseases appear to have biological roots deeply placed in genetic endowments.

One of the endowments that is universal in humans is the inevitability of a social context in development. The human being becomes what we think of as a human being as the result of a variety of socializing forces that predetermine language capacity, cultural traits and developmental possibilities. We all have them. What happens to us is determined by how these given factors in life are influenced by the environment that acts upon our endowment to direct that personal dimension of being which is everyone's own contribution to his life. This personal contribution has the power of life force, and the dynamics can be directed towards creative or disruptive goals as circumstances permit.

Let us now look at some of the elements of the social milieu that can affect life both positively and negatively. This treatment must inevitably be brief, for a book could be written about each aspect of these social conditions. But we can at least gain a brief view of how they fit into the total picture of healthy and unhealthy socialization, personal fulfilment or painful loneliness.

The family provides the initial and basic framework for personality development. When the family climate is secure, and the interpersonal relationships are based on healthy love and trust, the emerging person will have real advantages. The child who is greeted with love establishes supportive bonding with a source of security that can develop with the years. When this bonding and security does not exist there may be apprehension, insecurity and a tentative mood that impairs growth and finds support for negative attitudes. So the family is the basic unit for giving direction to the emerging life-force of the dependent child.

Interpersonal conflict in life may emerge from sibling rivalry or emotional inadequacy of parents. When it is wisely directed, the energy of the conflict can lead to an understanding of other's rights as well as a wise attitude towards strong feelings like anger. This may be a needed skill in coping with normal responses to restraint of the life-force. If, however, the interpersonal conflicts are unwisely managed, the result can be repression, guilt, hostility and an inability to cope with strong feelings. Then persons, instead of confronting them and talking them out, will be apt to retreat into themselves and lay the foundation for isolation and the mood of the psychic hermit. Interpersonal conflict is as inevitable as varied personal preferences, but the ways for managing it can be either creative or disruptive, depending on the skills that are developed in recognizing that personal rights belong to both you and me.

Neurotic interaction in marriage causes much personal distress and loneliness. We often wonder why it is that so many persons who have such admirable qualities in and of themselves appear to have so much trouble when they get into the close, constant and intimate relationship marriage requires. Part of the problem may lie in the fact that so little training is provided for this demanding relationship. For most people, the basic training in marriage is the emotional response to the marriage relationship in which the person was nurtured as a child. Statistics tend to show that the child brought up in a healthful home atmosphere where people trusted each other and could make adaptations as needed have good marriages, just as those who came out of neurotic or fractured backgrounds learn to break relations rather than adjust them, and retreat from problems rather than solving them. The present high percentage of marriage failure portends ill for the future, for the children of such marriages are learning a way of life that may lead to disruption and despair for them. A good marriage is not so much a matter of fortunate circumstance or some mystical quality as it is an ability to cope with stresses with competence rather than with conflict.

Most employed persons spend a major portion of their lives with colleagues with whom they work. Many of the tensions of life emerge from these enforced relationships where personal differences and economic advantage cause stress. Often the injuries inflicted in working relationships are so deep that they lead to venomous hatred. Then in-groups develop who exclude others from their socialization. The reasons for these exclusions may be looks, social status, education or places in the pecking order of the organization. Sometimes those who are excluded from association with those with whom they work have little else in life to relate to. The problems become acute when there is growing unemployment and this last meaningful relationship of life is lost. When retirement cuts someone off from work colleagues of long standing, the severing of these ties may produce loneliness and retreat into feelings of low self-esteem. However, inversely, happy, healthy working conditions can go a long way towards making life seem good. Instead of ulcers there may be enjoyment and anticipation of shared experience and productive activity.

Often the problems that separate people are the problems that are not confronted and worked through constructively. When a person retreats into seclusion with a problem, the problem usually goes along unresolved and complicates life more and more. The ability to make creative compromise and healthy self-assessment goes a long way towards resolving many of life's problems.

However, some of the problems of separation are caused by unusual community situations. Many people are caught in communities that limit or restrict life and growth. For instance, the life of the migrant worker has few roots. The children have limited schooling and are often excluded from stabilizing influences in home and school. What afflicts the migrant worker may in a quite different way afflict the migrant employer, who has difficulty relating to the people who work for him because the relationship is transitory. Fortunately religious and social groups are working to bring a new sense of community values into the lives of migrant workers and their families.

The penal community has a different set of concerns. The image of the hard and calloused criminal may be quite superficial as one gets to know the feelings of isolation and social injury that many prisoners feel. Some become increasingly embittered by their experience, while others find a new way of looking at themselves and at life, so that the period of temporary isolation becomes the seedbed for new and healthier growth. The society that penalizes its poorly integrated members may need to re-examine the practice of giving more isolation to those who already have suffered from too much. Menninger speaks of this problem in his book *The Crime of Punishment*.[1] To use personality-destroying techniques to try to correct those who have been deprived of life-supporting relationships seems irrational.

41

In quite a different way, the college community with its privileged status may be a place of personality growth or loneliness and despair. The high incidence of loneliness among college students is an indication of the frustration that may exist there. One study of depression shows that a majority of college students feel depressed quite often.[2] The major adjustments that must be made when a youth is taken from a sheltered and supportive home and thrust into competition with peers who pass judgment only on the basis of a person's acceptance in a new and different community can be stressful. Many students, however, look upon their days of initiation into a new form of community life as the most fruitful and enjoyable of their lives. As with most other forms of adjustment, the build-up of coping skills seems to be the essential key in managing the new and potentially threatening life patterns.

The hospital community also calls for rapid adjustment to potentially threatening situations. When one first enters the hospital there is bound to be some apprehension about what will happen. Will there be a physical crisis that calls for surgery? What will the results be? Will life be permanently impaired or will there be death? Such questions inevitably flow through the mind of the patient on entering this healing community. Those who are already there seem to understand what is going on. They have already adjusted to changes in personal and social values. The personal modesty that has so often surrounded many people is rapidly pulled apart by new routines and ingenious equipment for examining the body. The ability to make adjustments may be dependent upon the degree of trust that is placed in those who already populate the healing community. Those on the healing team need to realize that the problems of the ill or injured are not physical alone, and that the efforts to treat the whole person have beneficial physical effects. Apprehension, fear, isolation and loneliness need to be treated as well as an ailing body.

In recent years the military community has been engulfing many people whose lives are being recast in different patterns, with values, attitudes and practices that can produce separation anxiety and loneliness. The families of service men may suffer most severely as they try to live in foreign lands and different cultures. The effort to take along the habits and accoutrements of the homeland and build an enclave wherever the military goes may provide familiar items in the PX or NAAFI and familiar words in the offices and on the bulletin boards, but these may not go far in relieving the all-pervading sense of being away from home with its security and familiar ways. In recent years I have travelled much of the earth to teach techniques of crisis counselling to chaplains and social service personnel in military installations. I am well aware of the fact that our international obligations place a heavy burden on our nation's representatives. The more people are prepared to encounter cultural and social differences with appreciation and understanding, the less likelihood there is of the cultural shock that produces separation-anxiety and the pangs of loneliness.

In these various special communities that may be sources of loneliness it is obvious that one of the traumatic difficulties is separation from values that have been taken for granted. Most people are not too aware of the values that structure their living until they are lost. The loss of supporting values lies at the base of much anxiety. If values can be carried along and made secure, the anxiety part of the loneliness may be reduced.

With many people, the major problem of loneliness is heavily burdened with feelings of helplessness. The loss of familiar roles and functions produces a sense of uselessness, which in turn reduces self-regard and a secure status in our own eyes and the eyes of others. When this happens it may well be followed by the defensive stances that show up in irrational forms of misunderstanding and prejudice.

Basically, prejudice is a self-destructive method of protecting oneself against conditions that inject frightening prospects for the future. One of the most useful forms of intervention with the lonely and frightened is to try to change their attitude towards the future and its prospects. This may start with small forms of self-mastery and control of the conditions of life that may develop into increased inability to modify the future through present action. Expressing anger in creative ways, making sure that you are getting what you want in little things, is a starting point. Even returning unwanted merchandise to the department store is a step toward controlling the future. Ringing the bell to ask the butcher to give you the exact cut of meat you want is a step towards the form of control that can reduce hopelessness and start towards more careful management of the future.

Some of the more difficult problems that lead to loneliness, however, seem to come up against irreversible facts of life. This is true of bereavement, where death intervenes to change the present and threaten the future. Much grief is complex, but loneliness for the lost object of love is a major part of it. When it is impossible to change the outward facts in matters of life and death, it becomes essential to modify the internal perspectives on what has happened. No one implies that this is an easy process, or that it can be done quickly. Often it is a slow process of changing the perspectives one has on life. Grief affects the security system of the individual at the emotional level. The loss of a person represents the loss of a part of the self invested in the other person. The mourning process is built around the task of slowly but surely withdrawing the emotional investment made in the person who has died so that it can be reinvested in the future where the rest of life must be lived. Here the resources of religion are most useful, for tradition and historically satisfying utterances and ideas are used to reinforce a person's movement into the future. Even though it may be insecure and threatening, one must live in the future rather than in the past. The rich memories of the past can be carried into the future, but one cannot go back and rewrite yesterday's headlines. So the essentials of this process are a determination to face reality and adjust to it; to be kind to yourself while this adjustment is going on; to accept help and friendship from others during these painful times of transition; to fill the empty spot and repair the damage to life caused by the loss; and be willing to act out the deep feelings in the accepting atmosphere that is usually provided through ceremonial acting-out. The loneliness of grief is a constant in the life process, but when it carries the personal dimension its pain is so acute that the bereft need large doses of tender love and care rather than more isolation and loneliness.

With those millions of persons each year who go through the fracturing experience of loss through divorce there is apt to be a special type of loneliness. Even the anger and distress that led up to the divorce was a form of relationship. But when the break comes, there is often a type of grief, for something has died even though it may not be buried. Talking with many persons who have faced divorce I have found what seems to be a common response. Even though there may be relief concerning a personal problem that has become intolerable, there is a sense of loneliness. One person said, 'It is such a lonely feeling not to have anyone to argue with or yell at.' Another said, 'I think all persons who have just gone through a divorce should be treated as if they are sick for a year or so because we just don't seem to be accountable for the things we say and do.'

When divorce involves children, there is a double problem, for the children feel insecure and uncertain. They don't feel sure as to the direction in which they should turn for emotional help. Often they feel that in some way they are responsible for the problem, and so feel guilt in addition to insecurity. Often the impact of divorce makes the parent who cares for the children upset and less able to cope with the child's feelings and questions. The child needs a chance to explore the meaning of the changes and be absolved of responsibility. A number of useful books have been written about the needs of children of divorced parents. One that is especially useful in opening discussion is written by Earl A. Grollman, *Talking About Divorce, A Dialogue between Parent and Child*.[3] There does not seem to be any easy way to cope with fractured human relations. People put a lot of themselves into their love and friendship. They feel the hurt when it goes wrong. But there are some ways for coping with the break-up of human relations that are better than others, and these we want to know. People need to pay attention to each other's needs rather than to retreat into their loneliness further and further. They often need the special help of skilled counsellors to sort out their feelings and put their inner being back together again. This is true for children and adults.

The trouble with many fractured relationships is that they accumulate other problems along the way. The divorce calls for added responsibility at the very time when there is need for freedom from stress. There are feelings of personal failure and frustration that are hard to manage. There is the constant awareness of the absent presence that can have a special way of haunting life. And the mind races endlessly over the things that might have been and the things that may now be, as if in constant judgment. In addition to these forms of emotional stress there may also be changes in economic conditions that cause worry, and changes in living environments that further fracture life, for moving away is often part of the act of separation. When friends are needed most they are no longer near. So life becomes complex as crises accumulate. The lonely person is apt to find that loneliness breeds loneliness.

In order to escape from the possibility of becoming a psychic hermit it is important to work hard at the ways of reestablishing healthful relationships. The starting-point is always the attitude of mind you carry with you. You can be defeated by life and run away from it, or you can look failure squarely in the face, examine it and grow through it. Many people have found a new happiness they did not think was possible by refusing to let personal defeat be the final answer for their lives. Instead of becoming a sensitive, touchy person who amplified every injury, they worked to try to understand themselves, their feelings and the feelings of others so well that they could move beyond injury to understanding. Instead of becoming an insensitive and untouchable person, they could become more mellow, more mature and more ready to respond to the changing circumstances of life with healthy adaptation rather than with brittle hostility.

The person who can meet the circumstances of life that often cause separation and loneliness with a determination to grow through them rather than be overwhelmed by them will often find that the inner being can grow with adversity and become stronger by managing stress. Then events are things that happen to people rather than the opposite. The strengthened self then exerts its mastery over life, and life shows the positive results. At this point the values of religion may be most helpful in strengthening the inner being, resolving guilt and setting goals worthy of life's creative interest. To these resources let us now turn.

5

Loneliness and Personality Disturbance

For years researchers in the personality sciences avoided a careful study of loneliness. There may have been several reasons for this. Loneliness is hard to put your finger on in the laboratory. While everyone knew that this feeling caused great distress, it seemed difficult to separate cause and effect. Were people distressed because they were lonely or lonely because they were distressed, disorganized and lacking something important in their own natures. Some of the exploration of loneliness was exotic in nature: Admiral Byrd's adventure alone on the wastes of Antarctica became a best-seller,[1] and Henry David Thoreau became the patron saint of a cult that retreated into vapid solitude.[2]

But the study of what happened to real people in the throes of separation anxiety had to wait for researchers in psychosomatic medicine to take an interest in what made people sick and what could be done about it. Here illness was not considered primarily as physical symptoms but rather as the total performance of the individual in life, mentally, emotionally, and socially as well as physically. Way back in the middle thirties a remarkable woman named Flanders Dunbar wrote a book that was the end-result of her pioneering research in psychogenic and psychosomatic forms of illness. Here she equated frigidity with a deep inner loneliness that was unable to establish meaningful relations with others.

Dunbar writes,

> Frigid women like to be the man of the family, but when unable to achieve this, resort to a caricature feminity, calling themselves poor, weak women, and scatterbrained. They are usually very unhappy but they will rarely admit it until they come to the breaking point. Then circumstance or someone else is blamed for the break. They have a feel-

ing of loneliness, and are likely to weep if this point is brought to their attention or discussed. In lower social groups the girls usually get jobs, but give them up as soon as they get married because they feel that marriage incapacitates them. In the higher social groups they are likely to go to finishing school, become helpless, and complain of not being protected or cared for as women. Their husbands are usually 'not as good as daddy'. They are usually of superior intelligence.[3]

This picture of basic unhappiness and inability to find fruitful human relationships is the judgment of a physician and psychiatrist on the impact of existential loneliness on the behaviour of frigid women. When we realize that this was written more than forty years ago, before the advent of the women's liberation movement, we may question its validity. However, we need to recognize the fact that the movement towards liberation may have added yet another form of loneliness to that which already existed. The words used to describe it may differ, but the deep feelings may be the same. We note this contribution because it was an early recognition of causal factors in unhappiness rooted in a form of loneliness. However, the study of cause-effect in relation to loneliness did not stop there.

Fifteen years after Dr Dunbar wrote her book, another physician tried to understand what made some of his patients unhappy or, as they defined it, 'miserable'. He found that many of his miserable patients had developed ways of life that led them away from rewarding communication and relationships. They had developed ways of retreat from life and from other people as a way of protecting themselves against further injury from life. They were essentially the lonely ones. He found that they were usually bound up inside with fears and worries.

In his book *The Anatomy of Happiness*, Dr Martin Gumpert writes, 'A happy human being is one who can release a maximum of tension with a minimum of conflict and effort, and who does not suffer, either mentally or physically, under the continuous burden of tension and its release, which is the most vital quality of the rhythm of life.'[4] By implication, then, the unhappy or lonely person is in rhythmic imbalance, or simply out of tune. This may show up as boredom with a loss of interest in what goes on around, or a retreat into laziness as protection against being hurt by activity, or a state of emptiness where there seems to be nothing important going on either within or without. These barriers may be the defences by which a person protects the sensitive inner being from stress and strain, and the price that is paid is loneliness, or separation from life itself.

A more recent treatment of the subject has been done by a professor of psychosomatics at the University of Maryland Medical School in a book called *The Broken Heart. The Medical Consequences of Loneliness*. Starting with the loneliness of children, Dr James J. Lynch writes,

> Lytt Gardner reported a series of studies showing that children raised in emotionally deprived environments can suffer serious physical and emotional damage, including the permanent stunting of their physical growth . . . The psychiatric research clearly indicates that bereavement, divorce, sudden loss of love, lack of love, and chronic human loneliness are by no means felt only by adults. Children suffer from loss of love and lack of love even more than adults do . . . Dr Rene Spitz, now at the University of Colorado Medical Centre, first described more than 25 years ago the 'marasmus', or physical wasting away, of infants who suddenly lost their mothers. Spitz observed that some infants who suddenly lost their parents would refuse to eat and would eventually die even when force-fed. In one study with Katherine Wolf, for example, he carefully followed 91 infants raised in foundling homes in the United States and Canada. All of these infants were physically very well cared for. In spite of this care Spitz and Wolf reported that most of the infants appeared to be depressed, and many of them also seemed quite anxious. They did not grow as rapidly as other infants; they did not gain weight; and some even lost weight. Of the 91 infants studies, 34 died in spite of good food and meticulous medical care . . . [5]

We are dealing with very powerful and potentially life-destroying forces when we confront loneliness, even early in life.

The fact that loss occurs early in life, creating a climate of loneliness, may well plague life for years to come. It may show up in social behaviour. In his examination of vandalism and delinquency in England, Geoffrey Gorer found that the acting-out behaviour of overt destructiveness could be equated with the suppressed grief of children who had lost parents early in life and were acting out their anger at what they interpreted as abandonment.[6] Almost all of the acts of destruction were aimed at symbols of authority: homes, schools, churches and police stations. In a similar study, Rollo May examined in depth fourteen so-called juvenile delinquents and found that eleven of them had lost a parent or the parent surrogate in early childhood.[7] These unfortunate behaviour patterns appear to be rooted in emotional disturbances that cannot be coped with in the normal bounds of socially accepted behaviour.

But acting out the feelings of rejection and loneliness may be less costly to the person than those efforts to find psychological detours. Dr Lynch points out the long-range impact of isolation and loneliness in childhood on later psychological disorientation.

A wide variety of adolescent and adult psychiatric disorders have now been unequivocally linked to lack of parental contact during infancy. Hundreds of studies have shown that the lack of parental contact or the early loss of parents can seriously undermine the emotional stability of children. Severe adult depression, dependency, psychosis, various neuroses, and suicide have all been frequently reported among individuals who suffer early parental loss.[8]

Further evidence seems to confirm his feelings about the impact of circumstantial loneliness on the way a life develops.

Dr Roslyn Seligman and her colleagues at the University of Cincinnati College of Medicine examined 85 adolescents who had been referred for psychiatric evaluation from a general adolescent population in their hospital. They found that 36.4 per cent of these adolescents had experienced early parental loss (either through death or permanent separation), with the loss of a father being reported twice as frequently as the loss of a mother. The relative incidence of similar parental loss in the general adolescent school population was 11.6 per cent. Dr Glueck in the United States and Dr Greer in Australia have shown that adult sociopathy occurs significantly more often in individuals who have experienced early parental loss . . .

Another study of 12,000 ninth-graders from all geographic and socio-economic sectors of the state of Minnesota by Gregory in 1965 showed that adolescent delinquency rates and school drop-out rates were much higher for children who had lost a parent through death or divorce. Dr J. H.Nolan at the University of Maryland, who has studied cross-cultural evidence of schizophrenia, noted that over 90 per cent of the psychotic adults of the Loma tribe in Liberia had lost a parent when they were young.[9]

Not only does the loneliness produce overt acting out of disturbed emotions and the repressed form of emotional distress in life, but the impact of physical conditions has become explicit as extensive studies are made in medical research.

Examining the data from both the Middlesex County Heart Study and the Midtown Manhattan Mental Health Study, Bahanson observed that a significant number of fathers of coronary patients had died prematurely, usually when the son was between the ages of 5 and 17 years of age.[10]

A similar study was done by Drs Caroline Thomas and Karen Duszyski at Johns Hopkins School of Medicine.

They examined 1,185 Johns Hopkins medical students who had attended medical school between 1948 and 1964. All the students, while still in medical school, were given questionaires concerning their attitudes towards their family and the 'closeness' they had felt to their own parents. At the time of the questionaire, all students were healthy. Ten years later in 1974 the authors began to report on the relation between family closeness and disease. They concluded that those physicians who eventually committed suicide, had to be hospitalized for mental illness, or developed malignant tumors, had initially reported significantly greater amounts of inter-personal difficulties and had suffered from loneliness from one to 23 years before the onset of the disease and/or death.[11]

I recently finished writing a book with one of the leading authorities on the emotional roots of malignancies, Dr Lawrence LeShan. For twenty-five years Dr LeShan has been researching on the dynamics of so-called spontaneous regressions. This phenomenon has been observed under hospital controlled conditions. The cancer that has been developing according to its usual pattern appears to be arrested, not because of chemotherapy, radiation therapy or surgical intervention, but rather by some change in the body chemistry of the individual. The assumption basic to the research is that if these dynamics can be understood, they may furnish insight on new and valid forms of therapeutic intervention. One of the findings of Dr LeShan is that loneliness and the utter despair that accompanies it so often may produce changes in body chemistry so severe that the organism acts out its own self-destruction at those lower levels of consciousness that are spontaneous. The inverse may well be true, and changes in the emotional state of the individual may fortify the body's own immunological resources for combatting the neoplasts.

Caroline Thomas and Karen Duszynski sum up one of Dr LeShan's findings as follows:

The possibility that there are early psychological antecedents of malignant neoplasms has gradually been introduced into medical thinking as a result of detailed retrospective studies. LeShan's hypothesis concerning the emotional life history pattern associated with neoplastic disease is that early in life damage is done to the child's developing ability to relate to others, resulting in marked feelings of isolation, a sense that intense and meaningful relationships bring pain and rejection, and a sense of deep loneliness and despair. Later, a meaningful relationship is formed in which the individual invests a great deal of energy. For a time, he enjoys a sense of acceptance by others and a meaningful life, although the feeling of loneliness never is completely dispelled. Finally, with the loss of the central relationship, whether the death of a spouse, forced job retirement, or children leaving home, comes a sense of utter despair and a conviction that life holds nothing for him.[12]

Dr LeShan tends to equate acute loneliness with a loss of

meaning for life, a loss of direction and purpose, and a loss of some life-sustaining attachment that gave life security and significance. It is as if these lonely persons had over-invested in an emotional relationship which for some reason or another had gone bankrupt. He says,

> For these persons the loss of the central relationship can be catastrophic. The meaning and validity of the individual's own life may be catastrophic. For these people, in Pericles' words. 'The spring has gone out of the year'. Or as Shakespeare says in *Othello*,
>> There where I have garnered by my heart,
>> Whether either I must live or bear no life,
>> The fountain from which my current runs
>> Or else dries up. [13]

In his studies of the emotional antecedents of cancer, Dr LeShan found that almost invariably those who developed a malignancy had at the core of their being a mood of bleak and unutterable despair, as if the reason for being alive had quietly faded away and there was nothing left.

My own clinical experience verifies this. The breakdown of relationships may be related to unexpected forms of emotional support, not the least of which may be a pet. Let me illustrate. I was called to a hospital for a consultation by a member of the healing team. The patient in question was a 75-year-old woman who had recently developed a form of subcutaneous cancer that showed itself in little red blotches or bumps from the top of her head to the soles of her feet. It was explained to me that she had been admitted for diagnosis and treatment but that the chemotherapy was not to begin until the next week. After initial conversation with the patient, I asked her if anything unusual had happened in her life in recent weeks, or months. She responded immediately, 'Oh yes, my dog died.' So I asked her about the dog and she told me that she and her little dog had lived alone for nearly fourteen years. She said that they were good friends and that the dog could understand everything she said. She said they were inseparable, slept together, ate together and watched television together. It was clear that there was a deep bond of affection and a major investment of emotional capital in her dog. When the dog became old and feeble she cared for it, and when the dog died she suffered from acute grief.

When we talked about the dog, she responded that it was so good to talk with someone who understood. She said that relatives told her that she should not make such a fuss over a dog; after all, it was only an animal and they would get her another one just like it. But they didn't understand. She didn't want any other dog. She mourned an old and intimate friend who had shared life and given it meaning. We talked about the dog until she felt she had said all she wanted to say at the time, and it was agreed that I would come back four days later to talk with her some more.

However, two days later the hospital representative called and explained that the presenting symptoms, the skin cancer manifestations, had disappeared, she had been sent home, and the treatments were to be postponed until further examination seemed to warrant it. Over a year later there seems to have been no further manifestation of the subcutaneous cancer, and the patient has been able to establish new and significant relationships that sustain her emotional life. Each time I check on this patient I am informed that there appears to have been no further sign of cancer.

What does this illustration tell us? The patient expressed deep feelings of loneliness. As she put it so eloquently, 'I feel lost without Emily'. This lostness was real for her in her condition. Her security system was threatened because of the loss of relationship and communication with a constant companion. In describing cases such as hers, Dr LeShan wrote,

> These people felt a lack of any stable reference-points for themselves in the universe. There was no deep, solid emotional connection between the self and anything perceived outside of the self.[14]

We are told quite simply that when significant relations are broken and the broken heart results, the loneliness can have a bearing on all life: body, mind and spirit.

Now to return to Dr Lynch's study of loneliness and its medical consequences, we see that the broken heart is not just a romantic concept of the poet, but is rather one of the major causes of disease and death. The National Heart Institute estimates that the total economic cost of heart disease in

1976 was 58 billion dollars. We are dealing here with a larger item in the total American medical bill.

Dr Lynch says,

> If the lack of human love or the memory of earlier personal traumas can disturb the heart, then just as clearly the presence of human love can serve as a powerful therapeutic force, helping the heart to restore itself . . . Warm interpersonal support is a critical element in the recovery process of a patient.[15]

This is a physician speaking of the importance of love as a healing agent in life.

Dr Lynch goes further in describing why the heart attack has such important emotional concomitants.

> Irrespective of what might have caused the cardiovascular difficulties in the first place, the experience of an attack can be emotionally shattering. For many patients the sudden onset of a heart attack involves far more than physical weakness, dizziness, acute chest pain, or even total physical collapse; it forces many patients to reassess their lives . . . One day an individual is leading a full and active life, and the next day he suddenly finds himself flat on his back in a hospital coronary care unit, confronting the very real possibility of his own death. Much that was previously taken for granted must now be questioned. Can I return to work? How will I support my family? What about my favorite activities? What about my sex life? A heart attack is both a physical and an emotional trauma, and often the emotional scars are far more serious than the physical scars on the heart muscle.[16]

This emotional state often involves depression and a retreat from life. This often shows itself most after the patient leaves the hospital. Some studies have demonstrated that more than fifty per cent of heart patients experience depression, or a breakdown of their supportive relationships to life, and the more severe the heart attack the more severe the depression. In fact there seems to be a growing body of scientific evidence linking psychological depression to the development of heart disease, so it may be one of those chicken-and-egg phenomena. In the relation of heart disease to depression, which is the chicken and which is the egg, which is cause and which is effect? It may well be that it is both, for the intricacies of the developmental process may engage so much of life and its experience that they are constantly inseparable.

The impact of deep loneliness upon life then, is no trivial matter.

> The clinical studies reviewed indicate that both the presence and the absence of human contact may be critical forces leading to disease and premature death. An understanding of the relationship between health and companionship must include a recognition of the potentially devastating impact of terribly unpleasant human interactions . . . In this regard, the heart of human companionship clearly involves something that goes far beyond the mere presence of other human beings. What does emerge consistently from the clinical cases and mortality statistics reviewed thus far is that human contact is more than a trivial or incidental aspect of health. In many cases, it is the central issue.[17]

It is becoming quite clear that human relationships are of central importance in maintaining intropsychic balance and organic homeostasis. Whenever stress situations occur, the needs of the individual for security call for support, and usually it is other human beings who provide this something extra that life needs. Several studies show this. For instance, when patients who have been in an intensive care unit with constant supervision are moved into other sections of the hospital, they may feel abandoned by those who so dramatically shared their struggle for life. This may explain why there are more relapses than merely physical conditions would seem to warrant. The patient may be saying, 'I feel insecure away from your special loving care and so wish to return to it.' As protection against this form of reaction, members of the intensive care unit are often given the assignment of making visits to the patients in the other parts of the hospital in order to support and reassure them.

Similar studies in coronary care and trauma units have verified the fact that among those who have relatives or friends close by to show concern and support, the recovery rate is significantly improved. Sophisticated machinery can now monitor the effect of human contact. The tracings of heart action show quite specifically that when the nurse takes the pulse there is a calming effect. When a relative holds hands there is a lowering of the rate of heartbeat. Anything that breaks through the loneliness and isolation of the anxious person seems to show up in the monitors as beneficial.

Dr Viktor Frankl, in reporting on his experience in a Nazi prison camp, points out that those who could find some meaning and purpose in life improved their chances for survival, while those who could not develop some form of sustaining relationship mentally or physically soon moved into utter despair and loneliness, lost hope and perished.[18] In Lenigrad during the siege the radio station played all day and night just to let people know that there was life going on about them. In fact, the more important forms of communication and relationship often move beyond words and intellectualizations to simple human contact and the kind of deep knowing that cannot easily be put into words.

We hear much about the hazards of chloresterol. Yet Drs Stewart Wolf, Schottstaedt, and others

> used this metabolic ward to study whether human interactions might alter levels of serum chloresterol in patients suffering from heart disease in an environment where diet and exercise could be rigidly controlled. Their findings indicated that reassuring and supportive types of relationships could significantly lower the levels of serum chloresterol of patients in an intensive care environment, while stressful human interactions could significantly elevate chloresterol levels.[19]

The right kind of human relations seem to have a positive impact upon life and the will to live, even with the more severe forms of illness. Loneliness is negative, and right relations have positive meaning.

For some time we have been led to believe that the ill and traumatized need protection from human contact. The rationale seemed to involve several assumptions. First, there was apprehension about germs and infection, and that those who came in from the outside might contaminate the sterile atmosphere of the hospital. Further, there was the assumption that peace and quiet were essential and that those who invaded the protected environment might cause further stress for the patient. Also there seemed to be the idea that those inside the healing team could best understand the patient and manage his needs. In view of more recent research, these assumptions are called into question, and hospital practices are being re-examined.

While there are many still unanswered questions, there are some things that have become quite clear.

> By no means should it be concluded that human contact is 'dangerous' or 'bad' for patients. Quite the opposite. Human contact seems to be desperately important to patients in these acute clinical settings, and the heart seems almost hyperreactive in these environments to even the most ordinary type of personal contact.[20]

Those who are immersed in the routine of life in treatment centres may not be able to identify with the identity crises of those who are taken from their regular life-processes and injected into the hospital setting. The competent person who has not only been caring for all personal needs and also for the needs of others, is helpless and impotent to act. The person who has been confident and mature is now treated as incompetent and immature. The person who assumed authority over life now finds that all authority has moved into the hands of others. The complete change in life, values, and practices produces major identity crises in all the areas where Erik Erikson warns us to be aware of them.[21] First is the loss or threat of loss of someone important in your life-system, namely the self. Second is the injecting of new and threatening people and events into the life-experience. These would be the medical staff and the identity-destroying surroundings. Third would be the major changes in status and role relationships. The competent becomes incompetent, the mature person is treated as a child, and the control for life is taken over by others who assume complete authority for every life activity. These major changes tend to isolate the individual, and create feelings of abandonment when support is most needed. Bedside manner becomes important, for the patient is hypersensitive to the meanings of every word and action of the authoritative person who takes over the management of life.

The will to live then becomes important. Some surgeons refuse to operate when this depressive state exists in the emotions of the patient. Two friends of mine working at Harvard Medical school have established through their research that these feelings of loneliness and isolation from significant life-support persons can have lethal effects. Drs Thomas Hackett and Avery Weisman tell about patients who feel so separated from others that death becomes more appealing to them than the pains and burdens of life. They write,

> Death held more appeal for these patients than did life because it promised either reunion with lost love, resolution of long conflict, or respite from anguish. Each patient was emotionally isolated during the final admission. Their 'loneliness' was of different kinds: one man was a semi-vagrant who had never known emotional intimacy; another man had exiled himself from his family; one woman had suffered successive deaths of her husband and members of her family; another woman had repudiated all the most formal relationships throughout her life; a young girl had not only lost a close friend by death but was deserted by her physicians and family.[22]

These persons each had lost the will to live because of loneliness or emotional isolation. Each one died almost precisely at the time they said they would, and although there was considerable difference in their physical condition, there was a common feeling of being lonely and isolated. The will to live is fuelled by human concern and contact. When that is lost, the medical picture and the physical condition may become grim indeed.

What have we been saying in these last few pages? Until recently the clinical data on loneliness has been sketchy and incomplete. Now there seems to be a great mass of material that verifies the physical impact of loneliness in a whole variety of clinical manifestations. People do get sick because they are isolated. People do die because they are lonely.

In a postscript to his extensive study of the impact of loneliness on health, Dr Lynch writes,

> The full impact of the awesome destructiveness of loneliness, human isolation and bereavement does not strike

home until you look at brokenhearted patients 'being saved' by medical technology, lying all alone in coronary care units . . . These patients are not abstract statistics at all – they are old men and women, sometimes even young men and women, whose children have gone far away, or whose loved ones have recently died, or who don't know the names of even one person in their neighborhood, or who don't know who you should notify in case they die, and who lie in hospital beds for weeks without visitors. They are literally brokenhearted – there really is no other term to describe it – and something beyond drugs, heart transplants, coronary bypass operations, or artificial pacemakers is needed to save them. . .

The repair of a broken heart from the loss of a loved one may present far more of a therapeutic challenge than the technical skills needed for a heart transplant operation.[23]

But the insight of the physician who has discovered the meaning of deep feelings can be supplemented by some of the other forms of research that have been taking place in recent years that define more extensively the impact of this social epidemic that engulfs us. So let us turn to another area of research that illuminates the meaning and impact of loneliness.

6

Other Perspectives on Loneliness

There are conditions in life that would be ignored were it not for the inquisitive attitude of researchers who examine trends, put together statistics and assess changes in attitude and practice that affect all of us. In recent years they have looked at some of the components of loneliness that make it possible for us to see things in a different light. In the pages that follow I want to look at some of the findings of historians, social scientists, psychologists, anthropologists, economists and even men of letters to see what their more acute insights tell us about loneliness as we experience it in the late twentieth century.

Usually it is difficult for us to put ourselves in the place of people who lived a generation, a century, or a few centuries ago. The task of the historian is to recreate the past and its activities so that we can gain an appreciation of how our ancestors thought and felt about their lives. The perspective we gain from the historian's research may throw some light on the contemporary epidemic of loneliness.

Phillippe Aries, the French historian, has written with deep insight into the life and culture of the Middle Ages.[1] He has pointed out that there seemed to be no problem of intimacy such as we have with our preoccupation with individualism, its rights and privileges. Apparently there was no such concept as that of individualism just a few centuries ago. The lives of people were so enmeshed in work and social structures then that identity was achieved with no individual effort. People did not have to find out who they were. Their place in society was created and enforced by a structure so all-encompassing and so much greater than the individual that status was an unalterable fact of life. For instance, the person born into the feudal society was never in a quandary as to his role. He was the farmer, the soldier or the miller on the feudal estate. The woman was the one who nurtured young life and bore her share of the burdens of work.

In these times of which Ariès writes, all group life supported the process that gave members of the group their values and the meaning of their lives. Art, literature and religion were the unquestioned sources of meaning. The great cathedrals were not only places of worship, but centres of education, places for acting out the ceremonies that brought meaning to group life. Builders and artisans could build a whole life into the structure of a cathedral, and so they were one with what they built. There was no struggle for meaning, for the meaning was implicit and unquestioned. This was the way life was, and intimacy was built into human and social relations without qualification by any preoccupation with selfhood. The women working together on a great tapestry, the men working on a great building, and the children inducted into so all-encompassing a form of group life, were one in spirit and life before they could begin to make the distinctions that are so fracturing in unremitting selfhood.

Perhaps the distinctions so graphically drawn by Henry Adams in *Mont Saint Michel and Chartres* explain why he felt so much at home in the thirteenth century and so ill at ease in the twentieth.[2] In his autobiographical essays *The Education of Henry Adams* he makes the distinction between the pure and integrating devotion to the Virgin as contrasted with the disintegrating and enslaving submission to the dynamo.[3] The person could be elevated or fractured by what was the ultimate claim of devotion. In the thirteenth century, as Adams and Ariès recreated it, an essential intimacy pervaded all of life, and there was little or no struggle to define or develop selfhood as we know it today. Where intimacy was great there was little possibility for the separations that cause loneliness. The person was so immersed in inseparable relationships that there was no struggle to create them, and little chance for them to be dissolved. And in this structure the family played a secondary role. It was there, to be sure, but it was incidental to many of the other relationships of life that provided meaning, structure and forms of intimacy that were so implicit and taken for granted that they were more important than the other directions of personal development.

As I shall show more fully in a later chapter, the problems

of loneliness that are implicit in a quest for intimacy did not exist in a time when intimacy was basic to the life of the small and self-contained communities of that time. The self-conscious efforts to establish intimacy create quite a different setting for the human experience from those circumstances where intimacy was the unconscious concomitant of an all-dominating form of social structure.

With the breakdown of feudal patterns and the emergence of a new and different economic and social life, the family that had been incidental in the social structure of feudalism had to serve a new purpose. The individual farm or the family-centred craft became the centre of life. The family took on new characteristics, and often competition took the place of co-operation. Value systems emerged that were more concerned with comparison and contrast than they were with sharing. The uniqueness of individual families and their traditions grew in importance, and intimacy became an effort to establish self-satisfying relationships between families rather than the previous forms in inter-relationship, where social equality was taken for granted rather than achieved. Romantic concepts of favoured intimacy began to emerge, and families sought beneficial marriages that could enhance status and prestige. Intimacy then became an uncertain commodity in a newly emerging idea of the family as a power centre in community life. As more and more demands were placed on the family as an institution, the place of the artificially created intimacy became increasingly uncertain. And what was uncertain tended increasingly to become insecure.

For several centuries the power centred in the family was perhaps best illustrated by the royal families, who set a pattern of values for the masses of people. The superficial idea of significant human commitment so essential to true intimacy was flaunted by Henry the Eighth, and the last vestiges of artificially supported superficiality of the family as an institution was reflected during the reign of Victoria. Here the neurotic grief of Victoria was given acceptance, if not respect, as an essential to the manipulation of her emotions for half a century. During this time, when a facade of respectability was built around the family, its inadequacy as an institution to sustain life was showing up in the flaws and failures that increasingly undermined it. The ultimate example of this collapse of the traditional family came with the abdication of a king for a divorced commoner. The externally supported institutional role of the family legislated by law, social custom and the church could not overcome the inadequacies that existed in the institution which history substituted for feudal order. The twentieth century with its disintegrating family structure amplifies the problem that emerges when intimacy, identity and security seek their fulfilment in an institution that is inadequate for the task.

The multigenerational family structure that was characteristic of the nineteenth century was sustained by a combination of functions. Being closely tied to the land, it was an economic unit. It was also important as a centre of education, religion and social relationships. Elements of intimacy were found in this functional activity, for people worked together, worshipped together, played together and learned together. When anything important in life occurred, the tendency was to return home for the event. Children were born at home. Funerals were conducted at home. Life was centripetally focussed on the home.

But the twentieth century has seen major changes in the structure and function of the home. These changes have significantly affected concepts of intimacy, identity and emotional security. Here, of course, it is difficult to make clear distinctions between economics and sociology, anthropology and social history. Some of the major forces affecting the metamorphoses of the family are quite clear. It has been at the centre of one of the greatest migrations of human history, from the country to the cities. The changes resulting from this massive migration touched all of life, but the multigenerational family was a major casualty.

In place of the large family there emerged what is called the nuclear family. It has usually been made up of a husband, a wife and two children. In America, at least, it was characterized by a small house and a large garage, symbolizing the fact that when anything important was to take place, the movement would be away from the home towards other institutions that were largely impersonal, even though professionally efficient.

The nuclear family has been centred in cultural patterns that work to disintegrate it. It is pulled apart by the other impersonalized institutions of the community, the factory, the office, the school, the supermarket, the sports centres, and the churches. When both parents work, as is increasingly the case, the major investment of time and interest outside the home means that there is less where it is most needed, and tired parents want to retreat from relationship and responsibility when their children move towards them. The school, which can sometimes be far from the neighbourhood, brings children together with no other supporting ties in life, so even it tends to produce superficial and often insecure relationships strongly tinged with the impersonal. And when family members play together, it may often be in separate places, and differing interests have to be served.

Emotionally, the nuclear family tends to breed tensions and conflict. This is reflected in the large number of families that break down in separation and divorce, now about a third. Other families remain together in name but are shattered in spirit. Economics and concern for the care of children cause painful and often life-destroying compromise. The threats of death or some other form of dissolution of the nuclear family make certain areas of important communication out of bounds, and so the empty spots are filled with anxiety and stress.

Even those efforts to improve life conditions may boomerang. For instance, the interest in consumerism is designed to protect the consumer from deceit, sub-standard products and dangerous substances in food and other consumer goods. But what happens? As a by-product of this concern, a large amount of distrust is built up where life needs more confidence. So people become increasingly suspicious, and their apprehension is constantly fed by news reports and mass media articles, until the reader does not know whom to trust. Doctors, ministers, grocers and other persons upon whom the members of the nuclear family depend, are increasingly surrounded with the attitudes that separate. Where a century ago these persons were helpful and trusted friends, now they are increasingly approached with doubt and uncertainty, and the adversary mood takes the place of trust and confidence. These subtle changes tend to separate people rather than to bring them together in understanding and goodwill.

Looked at in terms of the sweep of history and the impact of contemporary forces upon it, it must be admitted that the nuclear family leaves much to be desired. It fails to nurture the basic needs for intimacy, security and identity.

The sociologist would assess the meaning of crime as a by-product of the fractured and fracturing nature of the nuclear family. A recent study makes it clear that the family is the most violent institution in our culture. Most murders are crimes of passion committed by persons who are related or closely identified in life. Assaults running into the millions are committed within the family. One of the major forms of child damage is the result of assaults by parents upon their own children. The research indicates that most battering parents have been battered children. Police dread the calls that often come to settle family violence, for the anger spills over on them and they are often assaulted.

Even this sketchy picture of the inadequate family that is characteristic of our day helps us to understand why there is so much despair, lack of personal fulfilment and insecurity in human relations today. The family that has been emerging from major migrations and economic needs does not seem to be the family that develops real identity, supports true intimacy and provides the surroundings for security in life.

Special forms of loneliness are generated by this change in family structure. For instance, the aging and aged who are sustained by medical advances in controlling infectious diseases have no place in the family structure. A century ago in the multigenerational family they could live out their days in a close relationship to those they knew and loved. Now that possibility is increasingly denied, and the homes for the aged and retirement communities call for a form of personal readjustment at a time when it is most difficult. The result is likely to be a retreat from life into a quiet and painful isolation.

The impact of the breakdown of the nuclear family is probably nowhere more dramatically portrayed than in a sociological study of health statistics for Nevada and Utah. These two states are almost identical in educational levels, *per capita* income and general climate and living conditions. However, the death rate in Nevada is one of the highest in America, while that in Utah is one of the lowest. There must be a reason. The President's Commission on Heart Disease issued a detailed report on efforts to conquer not only heart disease but also cancer and other diseases. It found that Nevada was unique, in that it had the highest death-rate for whites, and as far as women were concerned no other state even came close. Yet during the same period it had the second highest educational standards of any state in the country. It had the second highest median income, an average number of physicians and hospitals, and one of the lowest levels of population density. It would seem that everything here might be conducive to the good life. Quite the opposite was true.

Utah, on the other hand, a next door neighbour, had one of the lowest death rates in the country. What made the difference? Was it better water, more jogging, better food, or more tennis? In his study *Who Shall Live?*, Victor Fuchs points out that in Utah people are more religious, smoke and drink less, have more stable families, with less divorce.[4] Nine out of ten residents of Nevada were born elsewhere, whereas the majority of people living in Utah were born in their home state. The number of divorced, separated, single and bereft persons in Utah is about half what it is in the neighbouring state of Nevada. We have been taught that diets, medicines, inoculations and proper exercise are the best ways to ensure longevity. However, we may be overlooking the major item affecting our health and well-being.

> The idea that another crucial element influencing well-being is the ability to live together – to maintain human relationships – seems strangely unscientific to our age. Yet . . . loneliness and isolation can literally 'break your heart'.[5]

The break-up of the inadequate family structure provided by the nuclear home appears to be increasing with the years, and nothing that can serve as a corrective is in its place. Some extended family experiments, some collectives that return to the pattern of the Rhineland mystics, and some efforts to find intimacy without commitment are a part of the contemporary scene. But these experiments have not really affected the mainstream of life. The trend towards break-up and breakdown, isolation and despair through loneliness appears to be unbroken.

The roots of loneliness created in childhood are an increasing source of distress. In America, the divorce rate doubled between 1964 and 1974. In 1955 about half of the divorces were among childless parents or parents whose children were grown. Now parents seeking their emotional freedom are less concerned about children, and the number of children caught in the various forms of separation and isolation that divorce causes had increased three hundred per cent between 1953 and 1973. These are the children whose trust may be weakened and whose patterns for emotional problem-solving may be to move towards isolation and loneliness.

In efforts to find new and rewarding intimacy, the parents of children separated or divorced may move towards other relationships that further confuse the children. The end-result tends to be the psychological climate that is poorly designed to serve the needs of children seeking models of constancy and dependability. In their place they are likely to find the models of inconstancy, instability and irresponsibility. These again are the opposites of identity, intimacy and security.

Much of the quest for love and intimacy may well be a form of self-love where the efforts are not primarily to relate as mature people but rather to resonate, as is the characteristic of the infant or the infantile emotions of the physically mature but emotionally stunted individual. As the anthropologists who study human behaviour point out, there is a growing tendency to use other people for selfish purposes rather than to relate to other people with mutual appreciation and shared growth. Instead of developing skills in resolving problems of communication and relationship, the mood seems to be one of frantic escape into self-destructive forms of isolation and loneliness.

Philosophers try to stand off and look at the human scene to interpret what is going on. They also have something to tell us about the contemporary breakdown of values and the frantic acts of irrational destructiveness that are so obvious a part of our human relationships.

Over a hundred years ago Søren Kierkegaard looked at the forces of disintegration about him and was filled with personal despair and hopelessness. Out of this abyss of his personal observations of life he made a desperate effort to overcome his despair and find a source of meaning for life that could be ultimately dependable. Though he did not live long and had little impact on his own day, his influence has been strong in recent times, for he forced humans to be honest with themselves, confront their failures and seek both inner and outer strength to discover the ultimate meaning for their existence. One can only become a complete person when one seeks to be completely responsive to the highest goals for life. Values are nourished not through a selfish quest for personal satisfactions but rather through an intimate commitment to the highest one can know. Essentially his role has been that of the prophet who saw his compatriots taking the road to despair and self-destruction and tried to find another way beyond existential loneliness to hope.

The philosophers of meaninglessness who saw the futility and destructiveness of two world wars, ridiculed reason, gloried in the absurd and in so doing held up a mirror to life and life's futilities. Only when we can see ourselves clearly can we understand the meaning of our behaviour and the direction of our path to existential loneliness and despair. Captain Ahab and his Moby Dick no less than Kafka and his irrational trial are prophets of the futile search for meaning in the meaningless which only produces more destruction and despair. The meaning for life is discovered in its creative by-products more than in its frenetic searches. Intimacy, identity and security are not so likely to be the result of a desperate search as they are to be the by-product of commitment, dedication and what Jacob Needleman calls 'a sense of the cosmos'.[6]

The poet, like the philosopher, can point out the pain of loneliness.

> Little things that no one needs,
> Little things to joke about,
> Little landscapes, done in beads,
> Little morals woven out,
> Little wreaths of woven grass,
> Little brigs of whittled oak
> Bottled painfully in glass;
> These are made by lonely folk.[7]

And Rod McKuen, writing in *Lonesome Cities*, says in a few lines what long research studies hint at:

Sometimes I feel I've always been
Just passing through,
On my way away, or toward,
Shouting allelulias in an unseen choir
Or whispering fados down beneath my breath
Waiting for an echo
Not an answer . . .
And the empty heart that follows the
Experience of shallow relationships says:
And where are we now, where are we now?
A thousand miles apart,
What have we now, what have we now?
Not even love enough to break each other's heart.[8]

Or Chekov's Uncle Vanya lives out his empty life with the family whose futile communication about the trivia of life frustrated even the physician who tried to care for them all.

Or G.B. Shaw looks at the fragile loneliness of Saint Joan and measures as worst of all the isolation and pain of rejection by all she has known and trusted and given her life to save.

The artist, the poet or the dramatist takes the feelings that the personality scientist explores and measures and gives it flesh and blood and makes it move among us so that we see our own feelings alive and hear our own thoughts being uttered without our tongues speaking.

In the previous chapter we assessed the importance of powerful emotions as the psychosomaticist understands their impact on our bodies. In this chapter we have looked more closely at the power of loneliness to threaten life and health, change personality, modify cultural patterns and lay waste to life. Now let us try to move a step further into our confronting of loneliness by trying to understand our own feelings, how they develop, and what they can do to us if we are not secure enough to manage them wisely.

7

Loneliness and Some Responses to Life

Because loneliness can be such a strong emotional influence on life, it may produce unhealthy responses to the very resources that might be most useful. Years ago William James talked about the difference between healthy and unhealthy religion. Let's explore what he meant.

Religion can have a powerful influence on emotions. Religious perceptions are rooted in emotional responses. The religious response to life involves the deepest feelings as well as the most audacious intellectual assumptions about life. When religion becomes entirely a matter of feelings without the intellectual perceptions to guide it, life may be misled. Just as merely intellectual religion may be cold and austere, so merely emotional religion may respond to sick feelings and produce an unfortunate end-result.

In recent years I have done a number of retreats with many present who call themselves charismatics. Some of these people have found a new and warm dimension for a religion that had traditionally been forbidding in its major emphasis on concepts, ideas and intellectualizations. For them, their new discoveries served a useful purpose. For others, however, who were poorly grounded in an understanding of the need for wise judgment, their emotionalism tended to have hazardous implications. Often it led to distorted perceptions of reality, and if their sense of reality was already weak, their activity led them further away from the sense of reality they needed to strengthen. Under new emotional impetus the healthy persons seemed to become healthier and those who were already emotionally sick became sicker.

There seems to be a wave of simplistic religion spreading across the Western world at the present time. Most of this may be a response to existential loneliness and separation anxiety. Distressed people will cling to anything, no matter how unreasonable, if it meets deep emotional needs. But that does not necessarily make it desirable. Their second condition may be worse than the first, for they are further away from the type of insight and corrective action they need. To park your brains in order to satisfy your emotions does not usually lead to healthy results.

For instance, at these various retreats I have spent many hours in individual counselling. Two basic responses have consistently been revealed. The healthy response is usually described as a new and healthy drive to improve life, to stop drinking, to control anger, to achieve needed inner discipline. Here the basic needs were known and the new emotional strength served healthy needs. But often the opposite and unhealthy response was expressed. People would say things like, 'I was having trouble with my family and now a glorious thing has happened. Jesus has come into my life and I no longer care what my family says or does because Jesus is all I need.' In effect they are saying that the needs of the family have now been made secondary. The fractured relationships have been given divine sanction, and being saved is a way of escaping from the primary responsibility of life that the New Testament makes explicit in right relations with those who are closest.

I have attended many services conducted by those who follow this simplistic form of religion to try to understand the appeal they have for people of our day. One thing stands out. Although the ideas expressed are far from the insight of biblical scholarship and contemporary science, there is warmth and open friendship. Families stay together as a unit rather than being separated. The process is emotionally and socially integrative rather than divisive. People come together with good feelings and have those feelings supported. Much that they do is a needed corrective of arid intellectualism in religion, but there is no reason to believe that we are faced with an either-or situation. The finest emotions can be related to the deepest insights so that we move beyond either-or to both-and. Then we are able to worship in spirit and in truth.

The loneliness that produces unhealthy religion can also produce unhealthy social relations. People can come together to support the morbid dimensions of their living. The loneliness that brings people together at the bar to share self-applied psychotherapy in the form of a habit-forming depressant drug will perhaps find a temporary relief that creates a more severe problem as time goes on. Just because people come together does not of itself guarantee that something useful is bound to happen.

Useful group life is dependent upon the creative use of healthy feelings to create more healthy relations. The lonely person at a singles bar may well be creating more problems than are relieved. A person who joins a chorus, or an orchestra, or a string quartet to share the effort to create beautiful music, is likely to have a far more rewarding experience.

When loneliness creates depression it is important to understand what is happening so that the actions taken improve life rather than making it worse. Depression is an emotional state that makes life look bleak and hopeless. It feeds upon itself so that the more depressed you are the more reason you find for being depressed. Constitutional or organic depression needs special medical help. But the form of depression that comes with loneliness is most often situational, and the cause-effect factors are clearly discernable. We know what makes us feel upset and lonely but we have difficulty doing anything about it.

When that is the case, it is important for us to know some simple facts about our depressive state. The longer we put off doing something about it, the harder it will be to get started in healthy intervention. There are some things that can be done immediately. In a depressed state normal body functions are slowed up. The respiratory system works more slowly so that oxygen to purify the blood is in short supply. That is what tends to give the depressed person a pale or greyish look. The unoxidized blood shows through the skin. But this can be changed. Karl Menninger says one of the best things to do is take a long walk.[1] This stimulates the respiratory system, and purifies the blood and makes a person feel more alive and able to cope with life and its problems.

One day a student came to me with accumulated difficulties. His work had caught up with him and there was so much to do that he didn't know where to start. He was immobilized, and fretted about what would happen if he failed and disappointed his family and could not go ahead with his career. Instead of sitting there in the quiet office which might suggest even more threat of authority and pressures I suggested that we take a walk and talk things over. Several miles later when we returned to the office he had blisters on his feet but roses in his cheeks. Then we were in a mood to sort out his problems and make some initial steps that led to a resolution of what looked insurmountable. The mood of despair was changed into a mood of determined action by some simple expedients.

The depressive state so reduces a person's self-confidence that they are apt to sell themselves short. So it is never wise to make important decisions concerning self-worth under the weight of depression. The mood of depression tends to magnify obstacles as it reduces self-assurance, so a person is in double jeopardy. It is important to be able to understand the nature and impact of the depressive state in order to protect oneself from its negative influence. But it is also important for a person to gain insight into the dynamic processes in his own nature. Our susceptibility to depression and despair is a clue to what is going on within us. The more easily we move toward depression, the more obvious it becomes that we need to work on both our coping skills and our self-esteem.

The depressive state is essentially an illness of withdrawal. Karen Horney characterizes states of emotional disease as moving towards people in excessive dependence, moving against people in excessive aggression, or moving away from people in anti-social withdrawal.[2] The illness that withdraws reflects an apprehension about being hurt, deceived or abused. Trust and security are threatened and the moving away from the source of distrust and injury is the response. Erikson points out that this may start early in childhood in the conflict between trust and distrust. The abused child needs others to satisfy dependency, but may be injured by others who are abusive. The response is a protective stance that may grow into withdrawal when dependency needs are reduced, and this may be manifest during adolescence.

The uncertainty in human relations may set up an inner conflict that leads people to try to move in two directions at once and we get the phenomenon of the divided personality. Then there is movement towards people at one level of being and away from people at a deeper level of consciousness.

The neurotic person may show this inner conflict by projecting conflict into other human relations. So there tends to be deceit, divisiveness and trouble-making. Often this is done with such cleverness that the blame is placed not on the neurotic person but upon innocent victims of this destructive practice in human relations. Take a group of people who are getting along well and enjoying each other, bring a neurotic into the group, and slowly but surely suspicion, conflict, double-dealing and enmity begin to emerge. The social insecurity of the neurotic with deep pools of injury and loneliness projects itself outwards into the group and causes the trouble. This can show up in an office, in a club, a committee, or a family. Wherever it develops, it indicates an unhealthy use of a group process to satisfy the sick emotional needs of the maladapted person in the social milieu.

When a psychotic disorientation of personality takes place, the deeply rooted loneliness and disorientation in human relationships shows itself in non-rational behaviour. A person may act as if there and not there at the same time. There may be pointed attention that is a form of inattention. There may be accumulated and destructive suspicion that poisons communication and relationship. The paranoid person may feel constantly deceived and conspired against. The effort to move beyond this form of all-pervading suspicion may be difficult, for usually it is planted deep within the person and nourished by a variety of guilt-feelings that are manifestations of further social maladaptation. Sometimes the psychotic behaviour shows itself in an aggravated form of depression where there are alternating states of over-participation and withdrawal. In the times of over-participation there may be excessive generosity and poorly conceived acts of amorous or social relationship. During the other side of the cycle the person may withdraw so completely that there is little verbal communication and a blank and unrelated stare that symbolizes the whole pattern of behaviour.

The roots of healthy group life usually show up in creative and enjoyable activity of the group. The group may be held together by a specific function. This is usually the case with a work group, a military group or a committee in knowing that something useful is being accomplished and they are a part of it. Interest groups, on the other hand, are held together by some common shared activity such as playing musical instruments, collecting stamps or travelling to places of interest. The structured group is formed by a process in which the individual has little or no say. This would be true of a college class where a number of people have signed up for the same course, or a hospital group where patients are assigned to the same room and immediately are bonded by health interest and the hospital regimen. A therapy group would be carefully formed of a selected group to complement each other in working towards a specific goal. A heterogeneous group would be made up of people who did not think of themselves as a group until some special event amalgamated them in action. It might be a miscellaneous set of passengers on a plane who became a group when the plane had to make an emergency landing, and they were forced to work together to meet mutual needs.

The average person functions in a variety of groups almost constantly. It is when the individual is in trouble that the meaning of group activity changes. Some groups then may become threatening and cause retreat, while other groups may become supportive and give encouragement. So a person who is in trouble at school may want to rush to the security of his home. Or the person who has trouble at home may want to go out and seek companions who will listen to him as he talks out his troubles.

When individual needs are great, a person tends to seek out a group relationship that provides acceptance and makes the person feel at home. Also this group relationship should provide some form of status. Insecure people work to gain this group approval by such devices as buying drinks all around, or trying to be entertaining or even by trying to impress others with their mental or financial resources. These relations provide a temporary form of identification and self-assurance that meets the needs of the moment. Often during this temporary period some adjustments take place and some perspectives are restored that make it possible for the person to return to the group structures that have a more permanent place in life.

But people who have been injured deeply by group action may find that they suspect groups and want to relate primarily to individuals. This was true of William James, the great American psychologist. A biographer writes,

> The loneliness he felt was increased by the threat and oppression of evil. He reached out to his audiences, but for him life was an individual affair. What one could show was courage in the face of it, one's will to overcome obstacles. From groups, one could expect little. They were pompous, self-righteous, brutal; all the finest elements of life were to be found in the workings of individuals. James wrote to a lifelong friend: 'As for me, my bed is made; I am against bigness and greatness in all its forms, and with the invisible molecular moral forces that work from individual to individual, sneaking in through the crannies of the world like so many soft rootlets; or like the capillary oozing of water, and yet rending the hardest monuments of man's pride, if you give them time. The bigger the unit you deal with, the hollower, the more brutal, the more mendacious is the life display.[3]

This is a vital statement of the basis for friendship of individuals.

Yet even James would probably have granted that this retreat from group life and the romanticizing of personal friendships might prove limiting. It seems like the lingering echoes of the Romanticism that surrounded life a century before he wrote. The romantics might build an ideal friendship or love so unreal that it could not be realized. Then they would retreat into their inner recesses of being and carry on a love affair through letters, a secret diary, or novels that dramatized their emotions. This retreat into the self that denied the value of society or the possibility of reaching an ideal tended to be a form of self-love that further separated a person from essential forms of self-realization through human relationships. The communication was limited by its monologue quality and the essentially social being that had to retreat into an idealized perception of nature and his relationship to it.

This perception of the hazards of the loneliness that glorifies itself as romantic idealism is well characterized by Lewis Mumford.

Deprived of society, the ego loses any confining sense of its own proper dimensions: it swings between insignificance and infinity, between self-annihilation and world-conquest; between the hidden Sorrows of Werther and the visible triumphs of Napoleon; between the desperation of suicide and the arrogance of godhead. This nebulous reaching for illimitable goals was the result, in Rousseau himself, of his erotic limitations; that seems fairly plain. But the tendency passed over into other departments he touched. Isolation goes with such romantic self-absorption; and isolation in turn helps to create an inflated, suspicious ego, over-touchy to whatever approaches it from the outside, treating every claim of the real world as a conspiracy against the inner self. By tending to cultivate feeling beyond reason Rousseau lost the benefits of those sanative habits and automatisms which keep the social process in operation when feeling is dead and impulse has vanished: the duties of the parent and the citizen which extend the empire of love beyond the egos of the lovers.[4]

There may be some of this romantic retreat into the mood of loneliness as a response to the American value system as it estimates the quality of a person by success or failure. As the standards of success are largely external and material, the person who assumes failure is not only judged by society but by his own standards. This produces a double assault on the inner being and makes further retreat into the self seem warranted. Then it is but a short step to assume that to be lonely is a violation of the modern way of life, and loneliness then becomes a source of further guilt. Lee Rainwater in studies of poverty in America says that people who earn less than the median income feel poor whether they really are or not, and those who live below the emotional poverty line, who are sad rather than cheerful, who are lonely rather than gregarious, are likely to be filled with self-doubt and self-pity which makes their emotional condition even worse.

We have looked in the last few pages at some of the responses that are made to feelings of loneliness. Some people in their effort to work their way out of their emotional state move towards unhealthy forms of religious, social and personal behaviour. When they do this, they tend to compound their problems, for their efforts will be temporary at best, and they may then find themselves in a deeper state of despair and isolation.

Some people engage in defensive emotional activity that shows up in neurotic or psychotic behaviour, and they need special help. Some people even glorify their loneliness and make efforts to romanticize it. Some people move towards group activity without discrimination and so their efforts may not be productive. However, the more positive counterparts of the efforts to find the way out of loneliness may well lead to more healthful self-examination and wiser efforts to relate to others.

Dr Jerry Greenwald tries to help the lonely find self-perception by urging them to examine what he calls their toxic behaviour.[5] This is the type of behaviour that seems automatically to poison their interpersonal relationships. Among his illustrations of this poisoning type of relationship he points out the tendency of people to relate to others with comparable problems, with the assumption that misery loves company, but often the opposite is true. Sometimes lonely people try to help others by giving what they think is helpful advice, only to cause further complications in life. But the most common form of toxic behaviour seems to be found in the games people play. Here we are not speaking of sporting activity or amusement, but the games of make-believe, deception and projections of disturbed and disturbing emotional patterns.

Lonely people often play the most cruel games upon themselves, allowing themselves to be fooled by their emotions into states of self-pity, remorse and jealousy, and three more unproductive emotions are hard to find. On the other hand, loneliness can be a source of growth and self-understanding, healthy change and a development towards emotional maturity. These more positive approaches to the problem of loneliness will occupy us more fully in the chapters ahead.

8

Understanding Our Feelings and How They Work

Loneliness is a feeling, and feelings are of great importance to our lives. The first thing we recognize about a computer is that in spite of its ability to accomplish useful ends, it is incapable of having feelings. Feelings make people human. Feelings are both predictable and unpredictable. They are both rational and non-rational. But in spite of the fact that they are contradictory, they are nevertheless important, for they make the difference between being happy and unhappy, being creative and frustrated, being lonely or related to others. So it is important for us not only to understand what research tells us about the impact of loneliness, but also to understand that reservoir of feeling that goes a long way to determine whether or not we will be lonely persons.

Psychologists tell us that emotion is a complex state of the organism involving bodily changes and subjective feelings called affect. And affect involves the subjective feelings of love, fear, anger and loneliness that are a part of our emotional behaviour. The lie detector or polygraph is designed to reflect the bodily changes that take place when a powerful emotion is experienced. Most people are oriented about the truth, and when they violate it there are deep and automatic bodily changes so specific that they are measurable.

Some of these changes that can be measured are the electrical conductance of the skin which increases with the degree of emotional stimulus, increased blood pressure, more rapid heart-beat and changes in blood chemistry, faster and more shallow breathing, lowered skin temperature (often referred to as a cold sweat), reduction of salivation with a dry mouth, muscle tension and tremor, and other body functions that are more or less controlled by the autonomic nervous system. So a whole variety of things can happen under emotional stress.

Affectional bonds can help us to feel secure and good when

80

they are working well, and unhappy and pained when they are fractured. As development of the self and the full realization of our personal potential are related to these affectional bonds, it is important to try to understand what makes them secure and what can lead to fractured or fracturing behaviour.

What forms of emotional behaviour make friends? What emotional attitudes turn people off? What emotions can make people hate themselves? Perhaps we can best assess this varied behaviour by illustrating it.

Steve always seemed to have lots of friends. Most people thought well of him and responded positively in his presence. Steve was capable and had abilities that showed up in athletics, in a clear and active mind and in a well-developed body and an amiable expression on his face. But other people had these qualities without the capacity for friendship. What was special about Steve?

In the first place, Steve seemed to be secure in himself. He was never inclined to show off, take cheap shots at other people, brag about himself or his prowess, or go out of his way to attract attention to himself. He was rather quiet, but good-natured and loved fun, though not at other people's expense. So other people seemed to feel comfortable with him.

But Steve seemed to have a genuine concern about other people. When they wanted to talk he wanted to listen. He took other people and their feelings seriously, so it was quite natural for people with problems to move towards him because they sensed that he could be trusted and was really concerned about what was happening to them.

Steve also seemed to have a built-in gyroscope. He was usually quite well-balanced and not easily flappable. He believed what he believed, and although he was not one to try to tell others what to do, he knew his own limits and quietly stayed within them. So others turned to him for guid·ance and counsel. When they asked his advice he never told them what to do, but usually stated his own position and often said things like, 'I don't think that would be fair,' or asked questions like, 'Do you think that would be kind?'

Steve never gave the impression of being 'goody-goody', but there were some important qualities in his nature that seemed to make other people feel good in his presence. What were they? Steve seemed to know who he was and felt comfortable with himself. He seemed to have respect for other people and treated them with consideration and respect. Steve also seemed to have a set of values that were secure and unshakable, and while others did not always share them, they seemed to respect them and be comfortable with him because he was dependable. Steve seemed to have a relationship to something beyond himself that was so important to him that he would not violate that bond.

So Steve respected himself so much that he gained respect from others. He respected others so genuinely that they felt upgraded in his presence. He was governed by values so secure that others felt he could be trusted. He seemed to have many of the basic emotional qualities that make friendship possible. There was warmth, genuine interest and respect, and an openness that was willing to share life.

While we do not have space to explore how Steve became the way he was, we can be quite sure of several things. One, he was brought up in an atmosphere where values were important. Two, he was respected as a person, so it was quite natural for him to trust others. Three, he had always felt secure in the love around him so that it was easily possible for him to project the same quality of emotional security towards others. He had developed a capacity for intimacy in friendship, identity within himself and security in the relationships he had with others. He had the qualities that not only made friends but helped him to keep them.

Susan, on the other hand, seemed to have developed a special skill in turning people off. While she had an attractive enough face, her body was far from slim. She had a way about her that implied a constant attack. She was loud, and those who observed her closely said that she was pushy. When she approached a group of people she would blast herself into the middle, talking vigorously, with no apparent effort to find out what was going on and who was speaking.

When Susan was in a group she had something to say on every subject. Usually it was not relevant to the subject being considered, but appeared to be an effort to attract attention to herself and divert it from whoever or whatever else was in focus. She often tried to be funny, but usually her humour had a hostile or vicious quality about it that often brought it close to what her peers called 'sick'.

Susan liked to gossip. She would pick up information from one person or group and carry it to another with the opening gambit, 'Did you hear about . . .?' or 'You've got to hear this.' Usually people paid attention to her tales, but always felt uncomfortable about her because they did not know where she would be going next with whatever tit-bits of information she gleaned and nourished within her fertile imagination.

When people tried to protect themselves against Susan's hostile or threatening behaviour, she took it as a personal affront. Sometimes she would break into tears at quite simple remarks that expressed a contrary opinion. If in response to her gossip someone said, 'Oh, I can't really believe that', she would become so upset that her tears might flow or she would say, 'All right for you', and would stamp her feet as she turned her back on the group.

Even those who tried to like Susan because they thought they understood her problems were uncomfortable. She became smothering in her demand for total attention, and even her friends did not want to be so limited. When new persons came into town or into the college community she flooded them with attention and tried to claim their friendship entirely.

When men showed interest in her she was a strange mixture of gushiness and hostility. She could become jealous and angry at the slightest provocation, and when her mood was different she could shower her friends with what looked like affection. However, the more serious they became the more erratic her behaviour became, as if she was constantly testing them to see how much they could endure before rejecting her. And when they could take no more of her actions and left her, she assaulted them verbally in a most destructive manner.

Most of the time Susan found herself in a world of painful loneliness which she constructed for herself. Why did Susan act like that? Why did she seem to work so hard to turn people away from her? Why did she appear to prefer loneliness to real friendly relationships?

In order to understand Susan, we have to look at the major

influences which shaped her personality. Her parents were of a minority ethnic group that had a long tradition of feeling rejected. So they felt they had to fight for everything they had. They had a basic distrust of other people and showed it in actions, attitudes and in the conversation that surrounded the growing child. When Susan was five her parents had irreconcilable differences and divorced. For several years Susan's mother had a series of men friends who always made Susan feel that she was in the way. Even her mother made remarks that Susan interpreted as rejection, such as 'I'll see if I can get someone to take care of Susan', or, 'As soon as I can get rid of Susan I'll be there.'

When finally Susan's mother remarried, Susan was prepared to be upset with her stepfather. She tried to make things miserable for her parents and when she was punished took it as further proof that she was unwanted. When she went away from home she carried these attitudes of being unwanted and unacceptable as a person. So she tried to develop ways of making herself acceptable. Rushing other people and showering them with attention, carrying bits of gossip that she thought might appeal to other people, being loud and aggressive to focus attention upon herself, all of these ways of behaving became part of her defence against further rejection and injury. Susan had a lot to overcome as far as her background and self-assessment was concerned. The methods she used unfortunately made her condition worse. It was not until she had some skilled counselling that she began to get a perspective on why she was turning people off. Only then did she work vigorously to become a different person. When she became comfortable with herself it naturally followed that other people could feel comfortable with her.

It may be difficult to comprehend, but the basic elements of loneliness are learned responses to life. The neurotic person is usually in trouble with other people. A characteristic of neurotic behaviour is a reversion to early life patterns of behaviour. The infantile quality of neurotic behaviour is often reflected in comments that are made by those who observe it, like 'Come now, don't be childish', or 'You're too old to be throwing a tantrum.'

Why would anyone learn behaviour that would lead to the

discomfort of loneliness, separation and despair? It is not usually a deliberate process. It usually develops indirectly as a defence against something that is assumed to be even more damaging. The hermit usually retreats from society because it has been so injuring that he chooses his isolated and lonely life rather than face the possibility of more socially induced pain and injury. The psychic hermit does the same thing without taking to the woods.

It is at this point that we must consider the meaning of this thing we call identity. Psychologists use this word instead of the word love. The word 'love' as we use it in our culture means many things and often can be misleading. By using the term 'identity' to describe meaningful relationships, the ideas may be more sharply defined. We achieve our identity by a complex process of relating and communicating with other people. This process involves spoken and unspoken relationships. It involves conscious and unconscious responses to others.

Building identity starts so early in life that we are not aware of its beginning. Some scientists of personality development feel that it starts before birth and those who study genetics assert that we come into life with certain given qualities that we inherit from a long slow process of genetic formation. All in all, this process touches us in many ways, and put together tends to make us what we are.

The identity-creating process uses education, both formal and informal. The facility with which we learn language helps to shape our identity. When we have problems of communication, it may modify our self-perception so that we have built-in identity problems. Major persons who help to shape our body-image and our self-image even before we have any use of language are parents, brothers and sisters and those close to us in the family.

The processes of identification help us to learn how to speak, respond, get along with other people, show our feelings and enjoy life. If there are impaired relations, quite the opposite may happen, and we have trouble speaking and responding; people become threatening, and we are uncomfortable with our feelings. When that happens, we have trouble enjoying life.

As we develop through identification processes we achieve

85

a unique personality, something completely our own. No one else has quite the personality we have, for no one else has had the complex set of life-experiences that we have had. When all goes well in our growth, we develop a healthy and competent personality. But often conditions occur that create identity problems. We frustrate or offend other people, or they offend and frustrate us. All we need to do is watch a young child who has been roaming around freely and then has his freedom taken away by being placed in a restrictive play-pen and we know how quickly anger can develop and frustration be expressed. Life is filled with these restraints, and we learn to live with them, but in doing so we pay . price. We modify our identity by repressing our feelings. And because feelings have their own integrity and are powerful forces, the repressions may modify our personality. When we are frustrated, we may learn that a pleading smile gets better results than loud crying. These modifications started early in life may become so much a part of us that we never examine them unless some special event requires it.

The difference in the identity relationships shown by Steve and Susan tell us quite a bit about how their personalitie developed and their emotional needs were met. Steve never needed to cry for attention because he usually had it. Susan, on the other hand, had to fight for recognition and acceptance. What might have served her well as a child might not have been so useful later, but she had difficulty learning this fact of life.

One of the intriguing aspects of personality development is known as selective remembering and selective forgetting. Some of the problems of life are best managed by ignoring them, and others by confronting them. A child who cries for the moon must adjust to the fact that the moon is not within reach, and quietly forget the struggle for it. Selective forget ting, however, is not really forgetting, for the experience is registered and the response is also recorded in deeper levels of consciousness. If too many life-experiences become a part of this forced forgetting which we call repression, anxiety may develop. This may show itself in the feeling that much in life is not worth striving for because it is always out of reach Then it becomes clear that the emotional meaning of the events is misinterpreted. If the fact that the moon is out of reach is interpreted as rejection, it may become a focal point about which later rejection-experiences accrete until the feelings of rejection snowball and overwhelm life.

Identity relationships help to create the structure of our inner being. But when these relationships become strained in any way they cause identity problems. Any form of misunderstanding can create an identity problem. These are usually painful and cause aggressive action or withdrawal. In either direction it may lead to the loneliness caused by fractured human contact or retreat from other people.

Identity problems reach their most difficult form when an identity crisis develops. Here the possibilities for resolving the problem are acute. This may happen when death occurs and there is no chance to go back and change the things that might have been said or done. It can also happen when the injured emotions explode in disruptive acts and attitudes and a person says, 'I never want to speak to you again', or 'Don't you ever cross my doorway again', or 'From this moment on you are not my child. I disown you.' When emotions carry one so far that they say 'never', the pride and self-defensiveness involved make it difficult to back down and say, 'I'm sorry, I wasn't myself, and you know I really didn't mean it.' When high-powered emotions are triggered it is difficult to repair the damage, but because circumstances are difficult does not mean that they are impossible.

Intense identity relationships make a person vulnerable. When you invest in another, what happens to that other person is so important to you that it may seem that it is happening to you. When you love someone and they have good fortune, you feel fortunate. When something unpleasant happens to them you can feel distressed. When something devastating happens to them you can feel devastated. Love is always risky business, for the vulnerability you experience makes it possible for you to suffer injury more easily and more often. When the love is immature or misguided it may lead to jealousy or feelings of possessiveness that can easily lead to feelings of rejection.

When a person cannot tolerate the demands that love places upon life they have an acute identity crisis. This is when a person may say, 'Never again, I'll never let myself fall in love again.' This is withdrawal from life in order to avoid injury. It may not always be as explicit as that. It may be that people put limits on their willingness to give their trust and affection to another. They live in a no-man's-land of the emotions. They want some of the benefits of love, but they do not want to give themselves fully to the relationship.

A whole generation of young people are approaching life with this form of protective stance. They say in effect, 'We will share each other up to a point. We will live together and have the benefits of marriage, but we will not make any binding commitments. If we want, we are free to go at any time. So let's have fun with no fret.' This type of limited self-giving has built-in problems that cause a whole set of identity crises, for life does not thrive on tentativeness. The comings and goings of those who seek love without commitment can produce a deep uncertainty about love itself so deep and scaring that life is committed to a form of unresolved loneliness. And a brave front cannot easily cover up the pains of loneliness that become so much a part of the life that seeks identity without real identification.

The achieving of healthy identity relationships always begins with the self. The person who is insecure will reflect it in behaviour that may be aggressive or unreasonably submissive. The fine art of learning to love starts with a willingness to accept oneself without restraint or excuse. The New Testament tells us that the greatest commandment of all depends first on wise self-acceptance, for this is basic to accepting others and a cosmic purpose for life. But it does not say that this great commandment is easily achieved. It may involve failure and struggle for a type of self-mastery that is ready and willing to accept others as they are. But it cannot happen until a person is willing to accept the way they are without excuse, for this is the first step toward change. Defensiveness is a form of excusing that puts off the necessary work of changing. Love is a hazardous art, but life would be miserable without it.

So the question that we start with in trying to avoid the fractured relationships that lead to loneliness is not, 'Do we believe in love?' or 'How can I manipulate other people so that they will give me attention?', but rather, 'How honest are you willing to be with yourself?', or, 'How vulnerable are you willing to become in order to be worthy of love?'

When self-acceptance is achieved, then it is a next step to be open and responsive to others as a form of social acceptance. If we want to rebuild everyone else so that they conform to our wishes, we are inviting fractured relationships. If we work to understand others so that they are seen as they are, appreciated for what they have been able to do with life in their circumstances, then we are in a position to meld our experience with theirs and grow through the process.

Self-acceptance does not mean trying to be like everyone else. Our age of dress-alike, look-alike, even smell-alike is designed for commercial exploitation of style. This emphasis on the outside may often lead to a neglect of the inside where true emotional growth takes place. As it takes mature and healthy persons to achieve mature and healthful human relationships, the inner being cannot be neglected for a preoccupation with externals. Rather, a person may seek to develop unique skills for communication and relationship, and this may involve paying attention to others, listening to them so intently that the real self comes through and then deep may speak to deep and the foundations of friendship are built more securely.

The opposite of self-acceptance, of course, is self-hate. It seems strange that anyone would actually feel hatred against their own being. But this mood is probably more common than we realize. We hear it said, 'He is his own worst enemy', or 'Every time she opens her mouth she puts her foot in it.' These are common descriptions of the self-damaging forms of behaviour that act out feelings of self-rejection.

Growth in the ability to identify truly with others and express affection adequately develops when there is an ability to balance the pressure within with the needs without. What do we mean? Simply this, that the person must keep a wise balance between the inner being with its needs, and the outer beings of others with an equal awareness of their rights and needs.

Learning to be secure within oneself may not be easy. For some people it may be the most difficult achievement of life. It calls for a willingness to stand off and look candidly at ourselves, what we say, how we say it, what we do and how we do it. This is done in two contexts. It may be necessary to try to observe ourselves, our actions and attitudes from the point of view of those around us. What are their reactions and what must they be thinking? Sometimes this can be discovered by simply observing their responses. How do they react? What do they say? What are the expressions on their faces? What happens in response to the impact of one's person on other persons? Candour in this form of self-assessment may be quite revealing.

Then a second step may be an effort to listen more, pay attention more persistently. In this way we can get to know the persons with whom we work, play and associate. This effort to grow in understanding of others is not only an intriguing experience, but it may add a dimension to the possibility for true friendship that is important. When we stop trying to impress or manipulate others we may be on the threshold of a new and rewarding discovery. We may develop a form of depth perception into the natures of other people that will become essential to moving out of the restrictive living that so often characterizes loneliness. We may move into a deeper appreciation of others and their needs and abilities that makes possible true growth in human relationships.

Our understanding of our own deep feelings and needs is essential to identity growth and the capacity for living understanding that can break through the walls of loneliness. Our emotions are complex and sometimes baffling. But they are an important part of ourselves and we would really not want to live without them. The alternative is to work hard to understand where they come from, how they work in ourselves and others, and then we will be better set for the developing of the human relations that can satisfy life rather than producing the fractured relations that cause distress and the separations that produce loneliness.

Being a Steve or a Susan is not just an accident. It is the end-result of clearly defined processes of human development. When we move beyond blaming our parents or our environment for what we are, and accept the fact that we are the most important part of our own environment, we will then use our capacities for growth and change so that we can become the person who is worthy of friendship and human closeness. We will then be more likely to turn people on than turn them off. We will be more likely to achieve a creative vulnerability that is willing to be open and at the same time protected by a wise understanding of our own needs and other's behaviour. Then we will replace hurt and injury by understanding and positive response to others' needs. For after all, that is what friendship is about.

9

Loneliness and Identity

Just as developmental factors affect our capacity to achieve satisfying intimacy, so also circumstantial factors become important in achieving true identity. Here we are dealing with what makes a person assured and confident, with a clear sense of who they are. We often hear phrases, 'He is trying to discover himself,' or 'She acts as if she didn't really know who she is,' or 'As never before the youth of this generation are determined to find themselves.'

A physicist who is the dean of a great university finds an analogy for human loneliness in the black holes of space and writes,

How infinite the emptiness
Of black holes in the sky!
How deep the yearning of the heart
That's filled with loneliness!
Black holes are found in galaxies
Mid multitudes of stars,
And hunger grows within the hearts
Of people in a throng.[1]

In the infinity of space or in the mobs of people who crush in on each other, how can we find the essential meaning of our own being?

The essence of this chapter is that we can find our way out of the black holes of human loneliness only if we can first discover the wonder and meaning of true selfhood. Until a self is secure within this knowledge, there is little possibility that the self can discover other selves and see the light of being within self and others.

There is a strong probability that a person is able to find the self when the self is reflected in other selves. We know that identity emerges from reciprocal relationships, but where do the forms of reciprocity begin? Current studies tend to verify the assumption that intimacy early in life is basic to the development of true identity among adults; is dependent upon the ability to experience valid and mature forms of intimacy.

The development of identity through intimacy gets off to an early start in infancy through skin contact between the baby and the mother. The self-centred world of the small baby begins to enlarge when the identity of another separate being is established. When the mother with whom there is an intimate relationship is established as another being out there, the first great step towards an identity relationship is acquired.

But in our century there have been important forces at work to complicate this achieving of an identity relationship. In 1894, Dr Emmett Holt, a professor of pediatrics at Columbia Medical School, wrote a small book called *The Care and Feeding of Children*.[2] Its fifteenth edition was printed in 1935 and so for forty years it was the accepted authority on child care. It warned against too much handling or touching of the baby. It recommended that children be kept on a strict feeding schedule with no modification in response to the emotional needs of the child. It further recommended that there be no adult response to crying, for the child should learn to adjust to the adult world rather than expect the adult world to adjust to infant needs. There was to be little fondling and contact between mother and child, and the more quickly a child was safely on an impersonal bottle the better.

In fact this attitude almost became official when the US Children's Bureau of the Department of Health, Education and Welfare prepared and distributed widely a manual, edited largely by unmarried career women, called *Infant Care*. The mood of the little book can be sensed by a quotation. 'You may feel some resistance to the idea of such intimacy with an infant who, at first, seems like a stranger. To some mothers it seems better to keep the baby at arm's length, so to speak, by feeding plans that are not too close.'[3] With this approach to breast-feeding, the initial forms of relationship basic to identification are held in abeyance. In fact the major preoccupation of magazines like *Playboy* might better be called *Playbaby*, for they appear to be more a response to the unfulfilled needs of infancy than maturity, and the emotional bases for such a preoccupation with mammary glands must lie in some unresolved infantilisms.

It is interesting to see how these infantilisms have pervaded so much of our life. If one examines closely the major avenue of mass-media communication, one sees on the one-way communication of television a denial of the values of adult behaviour with a constant retreat to the forms of behaviour usually acceptable in children. Commercial television programming falls into four major groupings: humour, games, religion and news. Only one of the four makes a consistent appeal to maturity and reality. Much of the humour ridicules adults by making them appear stupid and foolish. Often the behaviour is non-rational, semi-violent to violent, with lots of shrieking and other forms of inanity, with the assumption that the need to laugh warrants this assault on the standards of adult behaviour.

Game programmes are very popular, with adults dressing up in stupid and childlike attire, and jumping up and down with childish exuberance, all for some prizes that are the incentive for the game-playing. This form of entertainment is interchangeable with endless sports events where millions of spectators are invited to invest their emotions in watching others play games. Seasonal sports move toward a climax in world championships and cup finals that release powerful emotions through the elevating of the experimental game-playing by which children learn to cope with life to the adult reversions that in effect ask for another chance to become children.

In America, the major diet of religious programmes calls for a reversion to simplistic childish thinking and acting, with clear distinctions between black and white and an emphasis on being born again as if seeking a second chance to go through the experience of achieving intimacy and identity with an all-loving, all-accepting parental figure. Usually the New Testament ideal of a second birth rooted in the achieving of an adult perspective on life and a mature value system is rejected for an emotional experience of being loved and accepted in simplistic terms. You do this for God and God will do this for you, with no regard for the mature perceptions that know you do not bargain in childish ways with ultimate cosmic reality but rather come to terms with it in

94

mature perception and stern self-discipline. In England emotive hymn-singing and undemanding near-sentimentality are all too common.

Whether or not we like to admit it, the only place where we find constant symbols of maturity on TV is in the news broadcasts. Here the newscasters who are most often seen and heard are carefully and conservatively dressed with precise language and reserved demeanour. Usually they give the image of father-figures, with an occasional glamour girl thrown in for bait.

Why this constant appeal to childish emotions? Could it be that there are millions of people who are trying desperately to go back and do some of the unfinished business of their childhood? That they would like to be babies, and would even be willing to go through the painful processes of birth again if they could find the assurance of the tender love and care that would get them started in the right direction toward intimacy that helps to produce true identity?

Other forms of infantilism that appear to emerge from lost intimacy in early childhood are observed in the treatment of psychiatric patients. Often there is a constant quest for a basic rhythm, a rocking motion among the emotionally distressed. Even though they may be sitting on a bed or on the floor rather than a rocking chair, this constant rocking back and forth is a characteristic action. Some observers even see in the strange and rhythmic movements identified as Rock and Roll a relation to this need to recapture the life supporting rhythms of early life. It has been established that the child rocked by the mother with the child's ear over the mother's heart is calmed and soothed. It is thought that the rhythmic action of the mother's heart so amplified during gestation produced a sense of security. The loss of this sense of security at birth needs to be supplemented in early childhood, or the unresolved emotional need may project itself indefinitely into life. In music therapy sessions, where the effort is to stimulate growth towards personal maturity and adequacy, it has been observed that patients move quickly away from the infantilisms projected in Rock and Roll and find their quest for maturity stimulated by classical music with its greater meaning and philosophical content. Even youths of the drug culture who have known no other music than the popular forms with the minimum of melody and the maximum of rhythmic beat, quickly move towards classical music as more satisfying accompaniment for their inner need to grow towards maturity and competence for managing their emerging inner being.

Another phenomenon in our culture which emphasizes the quest for identity that is basic to intimacy is the encounter movement. While it is difficult to characterize so diffuse a movement, it is possible to examine some of the major characteristics that are more commonly observed. Because I was an early contributor to the rebirth of interest in the inner being, and because my book *Understanding Prayer*[4] was recommended reading for many of the groups, I was invited to serve as a leader at a number of them over a period of ten or a dozen years with experience from Maine to California, yes, even from Europe to Asia. What I observed is, I think, pertinent at this point.

In a quest for intimacy, identity and inner growth towards security, hundreds of thousand of youths and adults felt that the small-group movement held promise for them. In this atmosphere of acceptance and common search they could discover a part of themselves that had always been out of reach and never clearly defined. Often they expressed it by saying, 'I have always had the feeling that there was something missing in my life. There must be more to life than I was finding. How can I find it?'

One cannot generalize about the groups or their methods. They ranged from monastic seclusion with its austerity and rigid discipline, to orgies that emphasized nudity and physical intimacies as a doorway to impacted emotions that had to be expressed in order to break through to the true self. At both ends of the spectrum there was a sense of the mystical, as if this dimension of life, so long denied or repressed, could only be discovered by finding a new approach to the inner being.

The prevailing mood in most of these groups with a serious intent was to extend the boundaries and skills in relating to others. There was a quest for global feelings, beyond hypocrisy and the value systems that supported war and the mythologies that supported conflict. The mottoes used often reflected this: 'Make love not war.' The quest was to find candour instead of self-deceit. Many of the exercises were designed to develop trust in place of suspicion and distrust. But the fallacy seemed to be that this desperate effort to programme emotions was not in tune with the basic needs of the individuals or their emotions. The method seemed to be borrowed from industry, the computer or the realms of commercialization. The feelings deep within people were seldom touched by methods or techniques of personality programming. Often people emerged from such experiences with further frustration, disillusionment and disgust. So those with fragile inner beings found their second condition worse than the first. A decade of desperate search for identity through programmed intimacy often led to an awareness that there must be another and better way to do it. Superficiality, infantilisms and manipulation, whether by a sincere group leader or an Indian guru, left unfinished business within the individual. How was that unfinished business to be approached? Was it possible for it to be effectively done?

The same emotional drives that led people to candour in place of deceit, and made them say that they wanted to get in touch with their real feelings and live in the here and now, can be used to discover true identity in the depths of being by substituting reality for illusion, and the sincerely mistaken quests of life for the more adequate and demanding disciplines basic to true love and true relationship.

Perhaps no one has studied the basic causes of alienation and despair with their opposites in true identity and social fulfilment more devoutedly than Erik Erikson.[5] His whole life has been focussed on what makes people develop into persons with secure role identification and inner security. He finds that in each stage of life the drives of the inner being can move in positive or negative directions. If the negative direction of life accumulates through the years, life will surely end in despair and disgust. But conversely, the earlier the positive influences are integrated into the growing personality, the more quickly identity will be surely confirmed and then intimacy and security should follow.

Erikson plots the positive and negative influences, beginning with the influences that develop trust or distrust. If trust exists, the forward movement of life can integrate experience about the positive pole of growth, but if distrust is engendered early in life, more and more of life's experience seems to amplify the distrust until it becomes life's major form of apprehension.

Next comes autonomy versus shame and doubt. The person feels secure and whole, or the inverse is true, and the person engages in self-rejection and uncertainty.

If shame and doubt are amplified, the next step amplifies guilt. But if a person feels a sense of confidence and wholeness, this is manifest in the ability to act directly, assume initiative and grow in competence.

If guilt creeps increasingly into life, there are feelings that cause self-judgment and the mood of self-punishment with retreat from life into fear and the qualities of paranoia. When guilt plagues life, the life is heavily burdened and it becomes increasingly difficult to move ahead with assurance and initiative.

Joy in creative tasks increases when the person is free to implement initiative with industriousness, but is limited when feelings of inferiority restrain the self from even the effort needed to try new tasks or assume new responsibility.

The better one feels about the tasks of life, and the more satisfaction there is in doing them, the more the role in life is confirmed and identity becomes secure, while the opposite is true if accumulated feelings of doubt, shame, inferiority and guilt inhibit the development of identity and produce what Erikson calls identity diffusion. Here the person does not have a clear self-image, and so plays many roles, even though they may often be in conflict. The weak person plays many roles without a central point for melding them, where the secure person is so sure of his inner nature that the varied roles in life are not in conflict.

When the person who has inner authenticity and a clear sense of identity moves towards others, it is with healthy needs and a basis for understanding and respect, because there is a basic self-acceptance that is free to accept others. If the opposite is true, the inner insecurity is a barrier to relationships, and so the person retreats further and further into isolation and loneliness.

When life is outgoing and creative, there is an inner mood that transforms the energy of life into positive action and a person is free to engage in the personal and social activity that is fulfilled and fulfilling. However, when the person is isolated, diffidence takes the place of action and the forward movement of life becomes bogged down in stagnation and defeat.

Then in the later stages of life there is little left for the stagnant soul but to feel defeat in life, unending despair and disgust with the failure life has become. So the ebbing years of life are filled with projected self-judgment that shows up in complaints, hostility, suspicion and frustration. However, the life that has been secure within and well integrated can enjoy the satisfactions that look over the past with appreciation and towards the future with faith and goodwill.

Erikson shows clearly the direction life can go and the emotional forces that can determine its direction. The efforts to improve the quality of life and reduce the personal and social pain and burden of loneliness cannot depend on legislation or exhortation to bring about the basic changes needed. Rather, there needs to be a process that can slowly but surely turn life away from its fear of intimacy and its breakdown of human relations that from the first day of life can determine the direction of emotional development.

This will call for a new definition of love. In our day it is so often thought of in biological terms, as if to make love were to define a sexual act. The concept of love that Erikson describes would be more akin to the idea of the New Testament that God is love, and the ultimate reality for human growth is found therein. When this concept of relationship is achieved, then those who dwell in love abide in the presence of the ultimate reality. This echoes the admonition of Jesus to start with the little children and forbid the destroying of their trust and self-assurance, for this impairs the development of true identity, and the inner kingdom is crippled before it is even aware of its sacredness or its potential.

Then the process of being born again moves beyond the simplistic quest for a magical formula that can absolve a person from responsibility for personal growth but will rather be the incentive to correct the developmental errors of the past and find a new self waiting to be born into full responsibility and full maturity. Carl Jung speaks of the religious needs for the emergence of true maturity. He refers to it as the second adolescence. During this period, when a person may have grown in personal understanding and intellectual maturity, there may still be a small-sized value system and inadequate motivation to sustain them through the middle years and the years that come along so quickly after the middle years. It is during this time that the failures of the past may be corrected and the unfinished business of living can be done.

In *Modern Man in Search of a Soul*, Jung points out that most of the problems of life from the period of the second adolescence on are essentially religious problems and the solutions will not be likely to be discovered without religious answers.[6] This is where motivation develops to move beyond stagnation and despair.

When Erikson talks about trust and the resources in life that can nourish it, he appears to be talking about what we usually call faith, a self-verifying process that takes the raw material of life, digests it in our spiritual perceptions, and then consecrates it so that it sustains and enriches life. It takes what might be destructive, and gives it the meaning that transforms it. The crisis psychologist sees the same experiences encountered by different people with quite dissimilar results, for what breaks one person makes another more wise, mature, mellow and loving. And it is not so much the experience as it is the quality of being that makes the difference.

When identity is achieved early in life, it can be nurtured through the years to form the best product of human experience, the faith-filled, God-conscious being. It is this achievement of significant relationship within the self without conflicting roles, with social acceptance of others and a feeling of at-homeness in the universe, that is the goal of the achieving of true identity. Then it is possible for a person to say, 'I know as also I am known.' When a person is free to love fully, there is little chance for the arid experience of loneliness. The person is too busy communicating love and understanding to project the inadequacies of being into human relations. The self that finds itself and truly knows itself is free to give itself. In this self-giving the boundaries that mark out the lonely provinces of life are obliterated, and the person discovers the meaning beyond words that is implied in the words 'God is Love'.

10

Loneliness and Intimacy

Earlier in this book we looked at the breakdown of intimacy in modern life and the sometimes frantic efforts to replace the lost relationship. Now we will look more closely at the present state of intimacy to see how we can move from problem towards solution, from causes of breakdown to possibilities for restoring health and fulfilment to human relationships.

Speaking of the plethora of superficial solutions that have been so popular in our day, Charles Frankel says,

> Most of these, it seems to me, do not bring peace of mind but only sleep. They confuse morals with morale, and self-control with self-hypnosis. . . It may be that it is only a passing incident in the history of a society that has been on the move, a society that has plenty of room for error and waste, and so has not been finicky about its methods or its moral economy.[1]

If the basic human problems of relationship and intimacy are to be resolved, it will not be by more superficial nostrums, more diet crazes, more weekend encounters or carefree orgies. These forms of juvenile behaviour may not be unexpected in a society that has only recently begun to look at human freedom honestly and human needs objectively. It has been only in recent decades that we have tried to assess people as people without regard to race, colour or creed. The children and grandchildren of human slavery are still to be found among us. The right of women to be considered as people first so clearly enunciated in the New Testament has become a reality only in recent times, and even now there is vigorous dissent among the privileged, who ignore the plight of millions of women whose rights and privileges are still restricted by ancient attitudes and personality-destroying practices. The movement for full human rights is still tentative and hesitant, with a long way to go before human rights are universal and we have a philosophy of history and human needs that protects people from artificial forms of isolation and social causes of loneliness.

To quote Frankel again:

> To see history without provincialism, to see all men and all societies under the same unchanging laws, responding to the same universal passions, beset by the same problems and searching in different ways for the same goals, and to understand all this without the help of sectarian revelation and without benefit of clergy – this was to have a philosophy of history.[2]

Our fear of the stranger and his strangeness, our apprehension about differences, has tended to place a restraint upon life that has made political and social capital out of isolationism both personal and social, and has created many of the problems that isolate people rather than bring them together in the tolerance and understanding that can create the foundations for a more healthful intimacy. We have seen tentative steps in this direction by the United Nations and the ecumenical movement among the churches. But differences are still suspect, and interracial and interdenominational marriages are still fraught with the attitudes that make intimacy difficult.

We must recognize that movement beyond the socially induced forms of loneliness and towards healthy intimacy is compelled vigorously to oppose the forces in our culture that seem determined to depersonalize, dehumanize and desensitize. For instance, the role of the computer may be quite useful in solving certain problems at the same time that it is creating larger and more complex problems. Human relations can become more trying when a personal letter to correct an error seems to have no impact on the mindless and emotionless machine that continues to deal with people as numbers and human relationships as outmoded. Yet the same machine makes it possible for education to be facilitated, accounts to be expedited and scientific advancement to make great strides ahead. The problem then is not so much with the machine as it is with the value system that makes use of the machine. It seems that our social perceptions were inadequate to master the machine, and so our immaturity in human terms was easy prey to the encroachments of the monsters we have created.

Even the toys we create for the indirect educational development of our children may be working against the goals we seek. How can there be greater intimacy rooted in commitment when our little girls are invited to develop temporary attachments to Barbie dolls that are to be traded in each year for new and more up-to-date models? How secure can love relationships be when from childhood they are programmed for obsolescence?

Several years ago I was sent as technical advisor for the US government to several other countries where there were large numbers of United States personnel, to try to assess the impact of the new moods of sexual freedom and the philosophy implicit in women's liberation upon the morale and social climate of Americans living abroad. While it is obviously impossible in a few weeks to gain in-depth insight into the deeper reaches of human emotion and personal practice, some things were clearly revealed. Among persons in therapeutic roles, social workers and military chaplains, there was a feeling that families were increasingly in trouble, that personal problems were increasing and that freedom as licence was improperly defined.

While I have long been in favour of many of the major objectives of the women's liberation movement, and Betty Freidan, who was a volunteer on the staff of the psychiatric clinic I headed at the time she wrote her book *The Feminine Mystique*, thanked me for the help I gave her in forming some of her ideas, I feel it is always important in talking about freedom to keep in mind the distinction between 'freedom from' and 'freedom for'. Always in the initial stages of social movements there tends to be overstatement, some forms of violence in word or deed, and a loss of perspective on the major goals to be achieved. There seems to be little gained in the forms of freedom that take over the worst attributes of those who would be opposed and reformed. There is little mood for rejoicing in phrases like 'You've come a long way, Baby', if the direction is towards ill-health, self-destruction and compounded problems rather than solutions.

Peter Berger and others make a telling distinction between

honour and dignity.³ They point out that a hundred and fifty or two hundred years ago people were strong on honour. It was such a major preoccupation that nearly everyone of status had a set of duelling pistols. Thousands of duels were fought over rather trivial matters of honour. The course of history sometimes hung on a few careless words that invited a challenge on the duelling field. Death often occurred. Then there came a day when duelling was replaced by a new concept – dignity. A person could confront a challenge by saying, 'Don't be a fool. Putting a hole through you won't change our attitudes towards each other. Why don't you grow up and act like a man rather than like a petulant child?' In that changing mood duelling lost face and became a thing of the past.

Something similar may need to be done to change the direction in which the need for intimacy is perceived. But instead of moving our quest for intimacy toward disgrace and disgust, it may be important to return to dignity and a new concept of honour. If freedom is to be really free, it must be rooted in respect for the best in human beings and the types of commitment and responsibility that can nourish that best. As George Gilder puts it,

> It is time to declare that sex is too important a subject to leave to the myopic crowd of happy hookers, Dr Feelgoods, black panthers, white rats, answer men, evangelical lesbians, sensuous psychiatrists, retired baseball players, pornographers, dolphins, swinging priests, displaced revolutionaries, polymorphous perverts and *Playboy* philosophers – all bounding around on waterbeds and typewriters and television talk shows, making 'freedom' ring the cash registers of the revolution.⁴

The careless freedom in the practice of intimacy reduces its meaning to the vanishing point. The concept of componentiality which is useful in industry and makes it possible to repair television sets quickly and easily by matched components does not serve the best interests of humans who are seeking true resonance of being.

Too often sociologists and other social scientists, like military commanders, specialize in fighting past wars instead of looking at the conflicts that lie ahead. The raw statistics tell us something about the movement of our culture where most crimes are committed by single men and the major complaint of young men seeking psychiatric help is their sexual impotence. Something is wrong in the way we are going about things. The *Playboy* philosophy which is centred on superficial forms of stimulation and chemically induced responses is essentially non-sexual. It denies relationship and produces the breakdown of human responses as a by-product of the retreat from the responsibilities of true relationship.

To quote Gilder again:

Nothing is free, least of all sex, which is bound to our deepest sources of energy, identity and emotion. Sex can be cheapened, of course, but then, inevitably, it becomes extremely costly to the society as a whole. For sex is the life force – and cohesive impulse – of a people, and their very character will be deeply affected by how sexuality is managed, sublimated, expressed, denied, and propagated. When sex is devalued, propagandized, and deformed, as at present, the quality of our lives declines and our social fabric deteriorates.[5]

Too often in recent years we have thought of intimacy as a commodity to be distributed by the equivalent of commercial enterprise, rather than achievement of the finest development and discipline of a human soul seeking to be worthy of self-realization and self-fulfilment.

The end-result of seeking intimacy in commercial and depersonalized terms is an abandonment of honour and dignity and a retreat into feelings of failure that are rooted in needs so deep that they can only be perceived in a religious perspective.

One discovers a widespread sense of pessimism and demoralization, a fascination with violence, revolution, drugs and the occult – and a strangely desperate loneliness.[6]

The escape from responsibility is reflected in the attitude towards children where women think it is fashionable to say, 'I'd never want to bring a child into a world like this', and the more privileged the education and cultural level, the more this form of escapism seems acceptable. The end-result is a form of self-destruction – social suicide rooted in self-deception and a glorification of perversion. In fact in recent years a new trend has been emerging in divorce court negotiations, where instead of fighting for custody of their children, women are increasingly fighting to escape from this responsibility, a further form of rejection of basic intimacy in the name of spurious freedom. Here the seeds are being sown for a new form of separation and loneliness.

What, then, would be a creative answer to the problems that emerge from intimacy fractured by a value-system that depersonalizes, a superficial group life that frustrates, a quest for liberation among women that tends to deny their essential nature, and a sexual freedom that makes true intimacy impossible as it makes deeper loneliness more inevitable? Some tentative answers are emerging in our culture, and while they may now seem fragile, they can become stronger as we work to strengthen the healthful and restrain the destructive.

These positive directions may be found in a new search for depth in life, a searching look beyond the first phases of woman's liberation by the very women who gave it its initial impulse, and a determination to redefine freedom, not in negative terms but in terms of positive discipline. Let us look more closely at the possibilities of these more positive trends toward true intimacy.

We are beginning to move out of an era when sex was the focal point of intimacy. The glut of physical sex and the efforts to be a gourmet in sexual activity at the physical or biological level is now being satiated. Just as most people can eat too much and suffer, and drink too much and lose control, so also too much of the superficial in sexuality can lead to emptiness, disillusionment and the raw material for a deep sense of loneliness. To think that one can discover the richest forms of relationship merely by engaging in a biological act would seem so illogical that it is hard to explain why a whole generation of people could have taken that route into disillusionment and despair.

In approaching any major social changes it is important to try to gain a historical perspective. The view of human history is probably given its longest perspective by the biologist

106

who studies the long, slow development of the human being. Dr Sinnott of Yale, a biologist, and Pierre Teilhard de Chardin, a paleontologist, explore the processes by which not only the body has been influenced by an evolutionary process but also the mind and emotions have been subject to a long and slow conditioning process that is built into the chromosomes and genes with such persistence that major changes in behaviour are fought by the inner structures of the being, in body, mind and emotion.[7]

The daring assumptions of those who would try to make major changes in human nature in one generation must be weighed against the endowment and inheritance that is built into every human.

When reforming the roles of men and women, we must always be careful to avoid behavioural gibberish – patterns of activity that so violate the inner constitution of the species that they cannot be integrated with our irreducible human natures. The problem of many of the sweeping new concepts of women's liberation is that, for all their technological feasibility, all their political appeal, they are sexually unconstitutional. . . To understand its full costs one must understand the woman's role in civilization, and feminists do not.[8]

The liberated woman's role that is well conformed to the basic endowment of women can have a transforming impact on society. Freud's unfortunate attitude towards women has limited the role of women in psychotherapy for years. Freud thought of the therapeutic relationship primarily in terms of seeking a father figure. But it is obvious that needs in psychotherapy may be satisfied even more by the ability to find a mother figure. The warm, tender, mothering role with the insights and skills of a sound therapeutic training may be able to advance the healing process more rapidly than the role Freud sought for male therapists alone.

While the nature and role of the nuclear family with its stress and tensions needs modification, it would not make sense to destroy its major redeeming factor, a chance for true intimacy and commitment, but rather to find ways of strengthening its mission by reducing the stresses and making it more secure as a place for healthful personality growth and real human fulfilment.

That there is a search for depth dimensions for living well beyond the depersonalizing, dehumanizing and commercializing value system that pervades much of life is reflected in the search for mystical meaning for life, a religion that is compatible with contemporary science and a growing seriousness among the younger generation concerned about their mental, emotional and physical environment.

Some of the problems of intimacy are space problems. Intimate space, personal space and social space seem to have been confused. Intimate space is reserved for those closest relationships of life, and a clear threshold to this intimate space is usually clearly marked. The relationships within family, then, are different from those within an office or a church. Social space is marked by rules of the road and courtesy that eases the processes of life, so that we do not usually slam doors in strangers' faces just because we do not know them, or cut people off the road with our car just because they don't look familiar. When the thresholds between intimacy and personal space are lowered, we can have serious interpersonal problems. One woman whom I counselled bragged that she had had sex with each of the two dozen or so men who worked in her office. She was trying to understand why things were in such bad shape at home with her husband and children. She was quite obviously having threshold problems. The breakdown of the relationship between the personal and the social areas of life can produce similar difficulties. The Klu Klux Klan and other similar groups try to protect false boundaries by building ethnic and racial barriers rather than developing rational thresholds that can be managed more wisely by mutual respect, courtesy and valid legal processes.

Many of the problems related to intimacy will be modified or resolved by re-examining the meaning of intimacy and the factors that limit it. So often people are afraid to express legitimate feelings because they are plagued by false fears. So a father stops kissing a son when teenage years are reached because he does not want to encourage homosexuality. Such ridiculous ideas may actually encourage abnormal forms of expressed intimacy.

108

The best way to develop skills in expressing feelings is to express them sincerely. Show love, express appreciation, and encourage openness and freedom of expression. Here the problem is not with the expression of feelings but rather with the value system that underlies the expression. Many people whose feeling expressions are impacted have developed irrational fears relating to control of their feelings. Nuns who chaperone school dances ask students not to get too close to each other, for they must allow six inches for the Holy Spirit. Religious restraints on the expression of deep and sincere feelings of affection have ancient roots and have been active in human relations for a long time.

At a Pacific School of Religion I am told that one half of the graduates now planning to enter the parish ministry are women, well trained, sincerely committed to the ideals of pastoral care and well endowed for this form of ministry. The problem seems to be that ancient fears stand in the way. Bishops have difficulty finding places for these pastors because some irrational fear still exists. The warmth and tenderness of a mothering role seems more threatening than the fathering equivalent. And in some other denominations the male clergy make most irrational judgments and utter inanities that reflect the fears that beset them. Perhaps the most ridiculous of recent utterances on the subject was that women should not be ordained as priests because they do not look like Jesus, even though no one really knows what Jesus looked like.

It is important for us to assess the non-rational and even absurd barriers that have been built up against the achieving of valid forms of intimacy, just as we confront the superficial and destructive efforts being used to find substitute forms of intimacy to satisfy those deep human needs that would move beyond isolation and loneliness.

The search for depth can help to develop an authentic inner being. This quest is essential as an antidote to the false values that have been thrust upon us by industrialism and its value system, and commercialism with its emphasis on giving value to the things that can be bought and sold. When we can have authentic people with inner integrity of being, we have the essential base for a value system that can stimulate and nourish true intimacy.

When the special sensitivities, tenderness and creative values of women can be appreciated, rewarded and fulfilled we may have a worthy goal for women's new-found freedom. While the exponents of women's liberation do not make any effort to see clearly what it will lead to in years to come, the current expressions of caution by its pioneer leaders like Betty Freidan indicate that the scientific studies of what the trends are is having some effects. A new sense of appreciation for the career of mothering is emerging, and the shrill calls for unproductive loneliness are losing their appeal.

The role of the housewife provides her a base for building a many faceted life, an opportunity few other vocations allow, because they are tied down to single structures and goals . . . Helen Lopata finds that housewives read more widely, maintain more close and productive relationships, participate more actively in community affairs, use their education more fruitfully and are far less lonely than those who are wedded merely to their careers.[9]

The new discovery is that freedom that is productive of the good life is not freedom from an inadequate past with its limiting values so much as a freedom for the future with a deeper sense of warmth, sensitivity, communication and productive relationships. If we are to work against the pall of loneliness that hangs over our society, we shall probably have to work deliberately and purposefully to learn how to grow in the skills of intimacy as well as in the value system that makes intimacy a valid part of life.

11

Loneliness and the Human Situation

There are those who believe that loneliness is part of the price one pays for being endowed with so great a capacity for perception. Plato thought of the human condition as comparable to a cave-dweller who was accustomed to darkness, but knew there was light outside. Moving towards the light was a constant impulse, like the moth burning itself in the fire, but the light for the human was so intense that it was blinding, so a retreat into the darkness was an inevitable defence. That produced only a shadowy view of reality.

There is something of this cave-like existence in all of us, for none is able completely to escape from the bonds of life's existential limits; we have magnificent visions and cannot achieve them. We have a sense of the infinite, and yet we are bound by finite bodies. We have a sense of the eternal, and yet are timebound in this existence. This is our existential state, and it can produce deep loneliness. Some believe that death is a deliverance from the timebound and finite existence into the infinite and eternal dimensions of our consciousness.

Psychologists would explain this as separation from the basic source of the energy of being. Ignace Lepp, the priest-psychiatrist, says, 'Psychic energy has its source in the collective unconscious.' When we are separated from the source of our psychic energy, we are in inner conflict that projects itself outwards towards the relationships of life. But it need not be that way. Lepp points out that the unconscious which is a part of the collective unconscious is not a monster but a serene reservoir of the energy that we can appropriate when we achieve inner wholeness. He goes on to say that in the primitive and the child

the domination of the unconscious is almost total. Neither the one nor the other is a monster, however, quite the contrary, most often they are endowed with a remarkable degree of psychic health. The civilized adult can share this same psychic health, provided that the assimilation of the unconscious by the ego takes place harmoniously, and the contact between the two is never broken.[1]

What he appears to be saying is that when the conscious direction of life is in conflict with its deep source of psychic energy, the person is sentenced to live in the darkness of the cave. But when the two realms are in harmony there is a new sense of peace within that can tolerate the light.

It is essential, then, to understand that the deep inner loneliness that characterizes our existential condition is not resolved by some simple procedure such as joining a group or playing games with oneself, no matter how pleasant and temporarily diverting that may be. It is accomplished by the processes of integration of being and depth perception that can resolve the inner conflicts enough to make it possible for the individual to come to terms with the insoluble problems of life. This is summed up in the prayer that asks for courage to change what can be changed, patience to accept what cannot be changed, and the wisdom to know the difference.

This is where the responsible adult achieves the maturity to manage even the poor start that might have impaired emotional development. What might at first seem to be a logical contradiction holds in its paradoxical grasp a greater truth. For we have said that the achievement of true identity, with its capacity for intimacy, can be started early in life and can grow into trust and creativity. That is quite true. But it is also true that the person who has had a poor start may accomplish major changes in perception and personality by directed effort. While we warn against trivial activities and inadequate perceptions, we would not obscure the possibility and the value of growth that changes the self and its orientation to life. This is one of the more optimistic possibilities for modifying both developmental and circumstantial loneliness. But these forms of loneliness are modified only when there is an honest facing of the meaning of existential loneliness. For until the self comes to terms with the individual's responsibility for change there is not likely to be any basic difference in the way life is confronted.

Part of the basic problem of loneliness is bound up with the prison of our senses. While our senses are wonderful windows upon a shared world, they are limited by our ability to translate our perceptions into the verbal symbols that make up our language. The best symbols always involve reduction, for the words we say cannot fully communicate the scene we see, the sound we hear or the thought we hold in the centre of our consciousness.

The skin is the boundary of the world of inner sensation and the world of outer experience. The eyes, ears, olfactory sense, the mucous membranes that govern taste and the sensitive parts of the body are all refined areas of the skin. The refinements of sensation that the skin is capable of achieving are beyond description. We can never fully understand the inventive-creative process that is at work to translate the sound waves moving through the air, into the convolutions of the outer ear, through the eardrum and through the three little bones that are so precisely formed that they are the only part of the body that is denied growth. They are the same size the day we are born and the day we die. From there they touch the auditory nerve, and an electro-chemical process transforms them into meanings that we try to express in words. But as there is sound loss with distance, so the sensory experience of hearing is inevitably reduced by the effort to symbolize it in words. Sitting one afternoon with Byron Janis, several of us were listening to him play the piano. He had just finished a beautiful Chopin prelude when one of the group said, 'What do you think Chopin was trying to say?' After a pause, Janis said, 'I'll play it again,' and he did. When he was finished he turned round and said, 'Now do you understand?' He would not try to reduce a work of art to inadequate words.

This inability of language to communicate what is going on in the depths of our beings is the core of our existential loneliness. Perhaps the poet comes closest to saying it:

The human soul seems doomed to live alone.
That which we share is but the threshold
Of the habitation of our being. Still unshown
Are the deeply hidden quarters which enfold
That which is truly us – these we don't disclose.

In crowded city, busy street, or country lane,
We move along our varied paths – touch friends and foes,
But unbroken is our wall; alone we still remain.

The worlds in which we live are also ours alone.
Though we may wish to share with you that which I feel,
To lend to you the colours and the hidden tones
My eyes and ears receive, no words of mine reveal
Even these simple things except in shadows faint.
I say 'the sky is blue', 'the music's sweet', and you agree,
But the meanings which for you and me these words
                                        convey
We cannot share. With words we cannot hear and see.[2]

But the same poet who feels that his feelings are so deep
within the cave of being, senses a wonder, a mystery and a
transcendent dimension of being that he calls the geometry of
the mind. Long miles of mountain, field, and stream now lie

> Between us on the surface of earth's sphere.
> Our minds reject this sudden jet-formed rift
> As thoughts reach back across the miles to hear
> In memory a familiar voice's sound
> And on mind's retina see a loving face.
> We cannot be kept separate or bound
> By ordinary pale of time and space.
> Transcending common sense – a mystery
> To those whose memories are dim – or blind –
> Distance in space coordinates and time
> Means naught in the geometry of the mind.[3]

The wonder and the mystery presses out the boundaries of
the mind to see the things that cannot be seen, to hear the
silent music of the spheres, and feel the closeness of spirit to
spirit as the depths are plumbed and the heights are scaled,
and communication takes on a new and deeper meaning.

One evening I sat for long hours with Dr Hugo Fricke, Nils
Bohr's first associate and the scientist selected to take over the
Fermi experiments at Argonne Laboratory after Fermi's
untimely death.[4] We were engaged in philosophical exploration of the meaning of human life in this cosmos, and it
was interesting to see how closely this stratosphere-level
theoretical scientist followed the thinking of Kierkegaard.

114

Fricke saw at the centre of life the suffering of the sensitive soul who could not sense all the meaning of his own being. He yearned for answers and sought a deeper meaning than the oft-spoken words seemed to give. If there was happiness, it was achieved in spite of this existential pain. If there was peace, it was in rising above the conflict.

As the hour became late and the philosophical musings became more abstract, Dr Fricke raised the question of the nature of the human spirit. Can this biological span of years be all there is to the unique endowment of the human consciousness, or was its energy preserved, as all other energy is preserved, in recast form and continuing experience?

Mixing quotations from Kierkegaard, the book of Job and the speculations of the modern nuclear physicist, Dr Fricke spoke of the wonder of creation. Then he repeated some of the majestic questions God asks Job in this ancient drama (ch.38):

> Who is this that darkens counsel by words without knowledge? Who shut in the seas with doors? Have you entered the storehouse of snow? What is the way to the place where the light is distributed? Can you chain the Pleiades or loose the cords on Orion? Who can send forth lightnings? Did you give the horse his might? Shall a faultfinder contend with the Almighty?

These and other questions bring perspective back into the mind of one who contended with existential loneliness. God reminds Job of his place in all that is. The series of majestic questions do not require an answer. They require an attitude. It is an attitude of relationship growing out of a clearer perception of the limited domain of man and the unlimited domain of God. Man's attitude of fear and frustration at what he does not understand is not good enough, for he needs a faith and truth that what he knows is a sample of the unknown and he can trust it.

The basic conflict of the nihilists who view life with suspicion and respond to it with frustration is the negative side of existentialism. Buber, Marcel and Tillich look at this unknown with faith and see a profound affirmation that can inspire the best within them because they are assured that the best they know is a clue to the nature of the unknown. This breeds security within, and their faith becomes a self-verifying fact, for when they act on faith they produce the fruits of faith.

After this discourse Dr Fricke opened the subject of immortality. He said that he was getting old and that the end of life and the nature of the spiritual existence seemed to become increasingly the centre of his consciousness. He said that the energy of consciousness seemed to be the most powerful and unique form of energy known to mankind. He found it hard to believe that this would be the only form of energy in all creation to be singled out for destruction. As all other energy-forms change without being destroyed, he had the feeling that the same might be true for human consciousness. Though he could not begin to imagine the specifics of this change, he was confident in its possibility and was willing to wait and see.

The basic questions raised by this profound scientist confront the boundaries of the human endowment of consciousness. If the consciousness is that part of the nature of man that is made in the image of God, then it is already assured that it has the mark of the infinite and eternal upon it. God would not be self-destructive, so the guarantee holds. But what do we mean when we speak of the nature of consciousness? It is more than sensory perception. It is more than mystical visions. It may be that in our understanding of consciousness we get a glimpse of the ways by which existential loneliness will be relieved.

It seems that consciousness is the mystical endowment of the human being that makes it possible for the various forms of reality to be brought together in a working unity.

The consciousness seems to be more than merely a by-product of thinking. It uses the products of thought to create a master perception of human processes to bring them into a holistic perception that makes the most audacious assumptions about life tenable. The consciousness seems to be able to bring together six different perceptions of reality in a way that produces something new which is more than the sum total of the six contributing parts. Let us describe the process.

The first three of the six realities are: sensory perception; the objective reality that is perceived; and the artificial reality that makes possible a working relationship which brings our assumption of sensory reality and the object of perception together in life experience. These three forms of reality are oriented about the so-called physical reality. The other three are related to the non-physical. There is the extra-sensory perception that is constantly at work in value theories. We know things that are not the product of sensory processes. This is supplemented by a transcendental form of perception that gives cosmic dimensions to our consciousness with its ability to move in and out of space-time measurements. And lastly, there is the mythic reality that takes all of our personal experience and brings it into accord with our racial and cultural inheritance. The end result of this appears to be the personal experience of what Alan Watts calls the 'supreme identity'.

Let us reduce this function of consciousness as the great amalgamator into an illustration. A man sits down at a piano. The piano is a physical reality and so also the man appears to be a physical reality. The man starts to play the piano. He uses a mechanical device to start air waves moving at prescribed frequencies. This, too, is physical. We say we hear music, and this is an artificial response to the physical realities, though it is the beginning of an adaptative process that moves beyond the physical. For we do not really hear the music. Actually, the music hears us. We only understand this when we move beyond the physical to the metaphysical. The sensitive equipment of the ear translates the vibrations in the air into an electro-chemical process through the auditory nerve and the brain into a meaning. Then it is that we can say we hear the music. Yet no one knows what really takes place in this inventive-creative process, so it is metaphysical and extra-sensory. But another step is possible, for the mind or consciousness can recreate the music without the physical counterparts. We can recall a Chopin prelude with no piano and no pianist at work. The mystery of memory can take the music out of the context of time and space and give it a transcendent life of its own in memory. And through the relationship to the mythic reality we can place it in its racial, cultural and historical place to give it a larger meaning.

In fact, Joseph Campbell feels that the growth of mental capacity is bound up with the ability to build greater myths as the growing edge of consciousness.[5] We see this through the development of the Bible. Progress in gaining new perspectives on spiritual reality came as the prophets repeatedly said, 'It has been said of old, but I say unto you'. Usually they were assaulted for presuming to challenge the old myths about which thought was organized. But the new and larger perception finally gained acceptance, and the new mythology was accepted until another prophet came along and challenged it with something larger and better. People resist the changes in their mythological loyalties, for growth is painful and adjustment to the new tends to be slow. The magnificent mythological structure that Jesus revealed to mankind is still too challenging for ready acceptance. The myth marks the growing edge of consciousness, and great myths demand great efforts before change is achieved.

This is probably nowhere better illustrated than in science and medicine. The theory of the circulation of the blood was rejected at first, as was the germ theory, and Ignace Semmelweiss was hounded to untimely death by doctors who thought it was ridiculous to think that they should wash their hands before examining a patient.[6] Madame Curie fought an uphill battle before modern science accepted the theory of radioactive elements.

It may well be that there will be an uphill battle before it is accepted that loneliness is a life-destroying ailment that is rooted in unfortunate developmental and circumstantial processes which must be corrected before there is a new and healthful life for contemporary persons. Those who propose a new value system that can undermine the values of industrial omnipotence, cultural manipulation and social impersonalization will face conflict and abuse, but the future demands that there be changes in perspective on the needs and resources essential to produce a good life for humans.

There will be efforts to defend science and materialism from the charges of failure. But William Irwin Thompson looks at Skinner's *Walden Two* and says, 'Frazier is a man who builds a culture that could never produce him, and a culture he himself could not live in as anything other than its creator.'[7] Even the high priest of behaviourism, William Miller, has been obliged to face its inadequacies and move beyond it in order to adjust to the discoveries of visceral learning. So changes are happening, and the ability of con-

118

sciousness to meld six different approaches to reality in a metaphysical process is already at work. Max Planck in his *Scientific Autobiography* says that no scientist can really be a scientist for long before he is compelled to become a metaphysician, and ends his book with the phrase, 'On to God'.[8]

In his book *Man's Search for Himself*, Rollo May says that 'the chief problem of people in the middle decade of the twentieth century is emptiness. By that I mean not only that many people do not know what they want; they often do not have any clear idea of what they feel.'[9] Then he goes on to say, 'loneliness is such an omnipotent and painful threat to many persons that they have little conception of the positive values of solitude, and even at times are very frightened at the prospect of being alone'.

These spastic responses to being with themselves are perhaps the most devastating manifestation of existential loneliness. Not only is there a philosophical inadequacy in looking at life, but there is an all-pervading fear of the self. 'Many persons suffer from the "fear of finding themselves allone",' remarks André Gide, 'so they don't find themselves at all.'[10]

We have looked at some of the human conditions that seem to predetermine an existential loneliness for mankind. But we have also looked at the breakthroughs that are being made by the philosopher, the poet and the scientist. They are not satisfied with imprisonment, and at least seek a form of psychic parole through their commitment to the mystical forms of reality that give transcendental meaning to the physical and sensory.

The consciousness-psychologists give us an important alternative to existential loneliness. Of the six realities melded by consciousness, three are oriented about the material and the sensory response to the material. In a sensate and material culture, that is where we live most of the time, and living there creates the problems of loneliness because we tend to ignore that other dimension of being which would move beyond the physical into the spiritual and the divine perceptions and attitudes that can help to make us at home in the universe and with each other. There are three dimensions of consciousness and three forms of reality that can move us towards this deeper feeling of identification with ultimate reality, rather than towards increased fear and alienation. Healthy religion has always tried to make the spiritual perceptions basic to life, and where they have been culturally achieved, life has been transformed for those who grasped the vision. The first-century church with its Pentecostal commitment, the thirteenth century with its fortunate combination of the insights, social processes and art forms, found another creative orientation for life. We may be on the verge of another period of spiritual integration and growth.

The basic mysticism of science makes it possible for the traditional mysticism of mature and healthy religion to find a new and creative integration which can move beyond the denials of nihilism to the affirmations of faith in the self, in others and the cosmic processes that undergird life. Then there will be the stimulus for creative growth rather than endless despair and disgust. Then we will be able to take the physical endowments and integrate them into healthy family living, and social goals that emerge from the awareness of common worth among all humans. The science that perceives the universe in mystical terms can then support the religious impulse, and religion warms the scientific endeavour. Then we will not have to park our brains with religious reductionism, but rather use them to create a new day of freedom for humanity, to realize its long-delayed goals: of faith which relieves anxiety, hope to destroy nihilism and doubt, and love to be a basis for healthy and healing intimacy.

12

Biblical Insight into Loneliness

The Bible is a source of deep insight into the human condition. While it can be approached as a book of history, prophecy, revelation or spiritual guidance, our interest will be primarily in its understanding of the human condition as it speaks about the problems of loneliness, separation and fractured emotional bonds in life.

The Bible speaks of the ultimate reality of life as the Word, the essential symbol of all communication (John 1); it personifies the Living Word as the power at work in life to help people achieve right relationships with each other because they have established right relationships between the inner kingdom of spiritual awareness and the outer kingdom of spiritual reality (Luke 17.21). In fact, Jesus implies that his uniqueness as a revelation is found in that unity that exists between himself and his God (John 14.9). In his teachings, he emphasizes the importance of right relationships.

Where mankind has tended to build barriers, he seeks to build bridges. He speaks of the temptation to develop violent emotions towards those who are close to us, and the need for reconciliation. In that remarkable part of the Gospel of Matthew called the Sermon on the Mount he speaks about the inner quality of being that transforms the baser emotions into the energizing power of God's kingdom in the inner being. He takes the primitive emotions that have to do with hunger and thirst, sex and security, and transforms them (Matt. 5-7).

So we speak of the deeper hungers that exist in life, and when satisfied transform human relationships. He makes fortunate or blessed those who hunger and thirst for righteousness. He takes the powerful drive of sex and purifies this energy so that lust is transformed into love (Matt. 5.27f). This love becomes the very nature of God, and he says that God is

121

love and that those who dwell in this loving relationship abide in the true nature of God (I John 4.8). He speaks of the deep injury that can come to life by fractured relationships and physical death, but here again the pain of natural grief is turned to a source of spiritual strength through the process of wise mourning (Matt. 5.4). Then even this sad state becomes a source of blessedness.

His ministry was one of reconciliation, of bringing people together as the basis for true worship of God. But it was not easy to break the old patterns, and often people chose the empowering influence of old hatreds rather than the new power he revealed of understanding and goodwill. Even two thousand years later the disruptive conflicts of his native land are a central problem for international relations. It would be difficult to find more specific utterances than those he addressed to the problems of hatred and the need for new and better human relationships (Matt. 5.34; 6.24).

For Jesus, worship was the developing of personal worth through a right relationship with God where the creature and the Creator achieved a true unity of being. There was only one thing that he put before worship and that was the achieving of right relationships (Matt. 5.24). He speaks of the problem of sibling rivalry that had so plagued the history of the Jewish people with murderous conflict between Cain and Abel and hateful deceit between Jacob and Esau. He knew how deep the roots of fratricidal enmity, conflict and violence could go. It took on larger dimensions through the group tensions that broke his native land into contending parts with the kingdoms of Judah and Israel. Unless these powerful drives towards violence could be curbed and human loyalties directed towards something higher, the future held more conflict and perhaps that ultimate form of sacrilege where human kind in vicious conflict would destroy the only God-conscious creatures from the surface of the earth. With the development of nuclear warfare and the capacity for overkill, that prospect is more real now than it has ever been before.

His response to the problems of this deeply-rooted sibling rivalry was quite simple. Where there is hatred and where there are insults; where there is false judgment and where there is hostile sentiment, there is the danger of destruction not only of the richest resource of selfhood, but potentially even of the capacity to know God. So the prerequisite of worship was to go first and do the works of reconciliation and then approach the altar with a purified life as far as human relations were concerned. And the logic of this process was simple and compelling: if we cannot love the siblings we know and live with, how can there be love between the creature and the unseen Creator?

In his living, Jesus illustrated the determination to heal human relations fractured by artificial judgments and prejudices. When he announced his ministry and preached his first sermon, he challenged the prejudices of his congregation, and when the sermon was over, they wanted to throw him bodily over a cliff to his death (Luke 4.14-30). When he confronted a hostile Samaritan woman at the well of their mutual ancestor Abraham, he broke through her hostility and shared with her some of the finest spiritual truths of the New Testament (John 4.4-26). Yes, his life was a constant challenge to small and life-fracturing thought and action, and a constant revelation of the power of love and understanding to influence life creatively.

Five illustrations that Jesus used clearly explore the dynamics of separation and the processes of restoration and reconciliation. First, there was the story of the woman who lost a coin (Luke 15.8). A gold coin in her tradition was a symbol of status and worth. It was often worn as a frontlet, a type of jewellery across the forehead. Apparently this woman lost one of her coins and was filled with consternation. She looked everywhere and could not find it. She became even more frustrated, and we can sympathize with her, for we know how a coin seems to have a mind of its own and can roll into the most inaccessible places.

The woman finally gave up her own efforts and decided she needed help. She called in her neighbours and they went to work in earnest. You can almost see them moving furniture that had not been moved in a long time and poking into corners that were seldom explored. The result of their joint efforts was that the coin was found. And then what happened? There was a celebration with rejoicing as the major mood.

Several important points are made by this story of loss and recovery. It illustrates the fact that there are forms of loss and separation that are not the result of intent but are accidental. Individual efforts to restore the loss may not be enough. There are times when help is needed. The frustrated woman was not afraid to ask for help when she needed it. With this help the lost was found. The major emotion that accompanied the recovery was relief and rejoicing. Celebration was the acceptable mood.

Often in life things happen that are not anyone's fault. There is no hostile intent. Accidental and unpremeditated factors intervene and take over. Instead of cursing the fates, direct and constructive action is taken to seek restoration. And it is strenuous action indeed. It is all-consuming in its effort. It becomes the only thing that is important at the time.

I was staying at a hotel in Los Angeles when a friend told me of an incident that had life-altering implications. He was registered as William Callahan. He did not know that another William Callahan and his wife had also registered. The first Mr Callahan had told his wife in Chicago where he would be so that she might call him if necessary. She did call, and had not made enough allowance for time-zone changes. A sleepy female voice responded and said, 'Mr Callahan, yes, he still seems to be asleep. Shall I wake him or do you want me to take a message?' The first Mrs Callahan, from her Chicago perspective, jumped to an unreasonable conclusion and responded, 'Don't bother, I've heard too much already', and hung up her phone. The second Mrs Callahan roused her husband and told him of what had happened. He said, 'This is bad. It could really mean trouble for somebody. Check the front desk and see if there is another Callahan registered.' They got in touch with the first Mr Callahan and explained what had happened.

The first Mr Callahan called home, but when his wife answered the phone and he tried to explain what had happened, she said, 'A likely story. Some cover up. How did you know I called? Forget it. Go back to bed with your sleepy female. She sounds very nice on the phone.' And with that bit of anger and sarcasm hung up again. It was then that the first Mr Callahan knew he was in serious trouble and needed help from neighbours. So he called the second Mr Callahan and with their aid cleared up the mystery, reduced the anger and restored the relationship that had been lost. It took effort, concern, a series of long-distance calls. But what would have happened if the seond Mr Callahan had said, 'That's not our problem. Some poor joker may be in for some trouble.' It's a long way from Los Angeles to Palestine, but the same principles are at work. And rejoicing can take the place of anger and despair when people work together to repair damage rather than ignore it.

A second story moves a step further in the exploring of the dynamics of separation. In this story the cause is not accidental but the result of carelessness and a preoccupation with other close-at-hand interests. The shepherd was out in the field keeping watch over his flock (Luke 15.24). But a hundred sheep are not easily kept in view at all times. One of them wandered away following his view of what appeared to be greener grass. Moving among the boulders and grassy knolls, this one sheep was separated from the rest. When dusk came, the shepherd guided his charges back into the fold. When he counted them, he was aware that one was missing. He knew which one it was because he knew his sheep by name just as they knew and trusted him. So after making the flock secure for the night, he set out alone to find the lonely sheep that was lost. Most sheep-farmers do not think of sheep as highly intelligent, and so without help they are not likely to eradicate themselves from the difficulties they carelessly wander into. Knowing this, the shepherd made haste to seek and save what was lost through carelessness.

Out into the night he went, wandering through the treacherous desert country with its steep cliffs and boulder-strewn waddies. As he went, he stopped and listened for any bleating that could lead him to the lost sheep. After some searching, scratches, bruises and falls he located the errant animal and, carrying it on his shoulders, reassured it and took it back to the safety of the fold. Then, like the woman who had found her lost coin, he rejoiced. The fractured relationships, the hazardous aloneness, the threatening isolation had been overcome. Identity, intimacy and security took the place of lostness, separation from its own kind and its plight as easy prey for predators. With seventy per cent of our population living in cities nowadays there are not many who would easily relate to this story of the shepherd and his sheep, but the human conditions it illustrates are ever recurring.

Kim Yil Chyung had come from Korea to study journalism. He had a brilliant mind but little money. When the school term was over he went to New York to seek summer work. He registered at the International House. Then he seemed to drop from sight. His friends heard nothing from him. One friend who had tutored Kim in English began to have an almost constant image of Kim in his thoughts and even in his dreams. But at first he tried to push them aside because he said to himself that if Kim needed him he would certainly get in touch. However, the image persisted, and so one Sunday afternoon this friend took a train to New York and made inquiry at the International House about his friend Kim. There he found that he was registered with an address, but no one had seen him for a couple of weeks.

So Kim's friend sought him out. He went to the fifth floor of a rather shabby walk-up tenement, and after searching in the semi-darkness and finding no names, decided to knock on all the doors. He was told that there was a Korean-looking man in apartment 5F. In response to repeated knocks there was finally a feeble response, 'Come in.' Soon a story emerged. Kim had not been able to get work. He used up his money. He could not buy food and he was too proud to beg. He became weaker until he was not able to travel up and down the stairs. He retreated to his meagrely furnished room and to its bed. Helpless to act or even to call for help, he was slowly starving to death. His friend immediately went out and bought chicken and beef broth, and started the process of nourishing the famished body. Then he summoned emergency medical help and notified other Korean students registered at the International House. In a few weeks Kim was restored to health of body, and his despair and helplessness were overcome as friends cared for him and prepared him for his return to college in the fall. After returning home, Kim became a useful leader in his church and community.

Often a friend can play the role of a shepherd, moving towards those who have carelessly let the life-sustaining lines of communication break down. In the midst of great cities there is the constant threat of getting lost, and the loneliness that results cannot usually be overcome without the co-operation of someone who is concerned enough to run some risks, make some sacrifices and vigorously listen for and search out those who cannot make it on their own.

The third story Jesus tells has to do with a deliberate and wilful effort to fracture the bonds that have nurtured life (Luke 15.11-25). It is a fascinating and perceptive insight into adolescent psychology. A father had two sons, quite different in their personalities. One was passive and submissive and the other quite rebellious and hard to manage. One day this son with the turbulent personality confronted his father and said something like this. 'Father, this place is getting me down. Nothing every happens here. There is a great big world out there. I'd like to live a little. You've got plenty. How about giving me some of what is coming to me eventually, and let me try to make it on my own.' We don't know what the father said, but we know that finally he acquiesced and gave his son part of his inheritance. So the son collected some things and went off. The father was disturbed. He knew something of the world and its pressures, but he couldn't follow along to protect his son. He had to let him go his way. But he wondered and prayed and watched out of the window.

The son, on the other hand, found people who had a taste for the good life, and as long as there was money around they were willing to share it. So there was a time of fun and activity, riotous living. But the money began to be scarce, and then ran out. Jobs were few, and soon our young man was reduced to the most menial of occupations, a swine herder. He even came to the place where he was so hungry that he ate the husks that were thrown to the pigs. Then one day there was a burst of insight, the sort of thing that may happen to a teenager who acquires perspective on himself and his world. In briefer terms, he came to himself. He thought, the servants in my father's house are better off than I am. They eat and sleep well and have decent clothes to wear. What am I doing here? I could go home and at least get work as a servant. So he started his way on the journey back to life-sustaining relationship. His father, watching out of the window, saw a familiar figure in the distance, and instead of waiting for his arrival ran towards his son and embraced him with sincere expressions of love.

Instead of saying, 'I knew you would make a fool of yourself. I hope you have learned your lesson,' the father showered him with the evidences of acceptance. He said, 'come in and have a shower, put on some fresh clothes, get rid of those smelly rags, and let's have a party. We will kill a fatted calf and have a barbecue with music and dancing.' He too, wanted to rejoice, but not so the son who had stayed at home and felt that at last he had his father all to himself. His jealousy came to the surface and he lamented the fact that he had never had a party like this.

The father tried to explain that sustained relationships have their own rewards by helping to keep life secure, but that when relations have been broken, even deliberately, there is cause for rejoicing when they are restored. It was hard for this jealous son to get the idea that love is something given, rather than something bargained for. He sulked during the party.

This classic lesson in adolescent psychology points out that the efforts to grow up into mature self-assurance and responsibility for life may not be a smooth and easy process. It may be tough and turbulent, and call for lots of parental understanding and patience. But the wise parent knows what is happening, and stands by ready to restore the relationships that are so easily broken during this time of life.

John was seventeen and a senior in high school when his family bought a new car. He liked its new lines and its acceleration. He wanted to show off this new car to his friends, especially his girl friend. He had a licence to drive and thought he was able to manage any car. When his father was at the office and his mother at a meeting, he backed the car out and took it for a trial run. Naturally he made sure that his girl friend was along to admire the car and his ability to handle it. They both knew instinctively that a car is the prized symbol of maturity in our culture, and a teenager wants to look and act mature. That's what the whole process of growing up is all about.

But it didn't turn out quite as John had hoped. Trying to pass a slow-moving car and do a little showing off at the same time, he side-swiped another and caused considerable damage to both cars. The police were called and made a report of the damage and charged John with careless driving. When John called from the police station, his father was primarily concerned about the possibility of personal injury. When he found that both John and his girl friend, though shaken up and emotionally distressed, were uninjured, he expressed joy and said he was to wait and he would be right over. There was no recrimination and no sermons. John's father seemed to sense that John already had more guilt feelings than he could manage. So his father gave reassurance about the insurance that would cover the damage, and continued to express his joy that there was no personal injury. He pointed out that new cars were replaceable, but not people. John did not have to protect his injured feelings by protecting himself against parental judgment. Rather, he could use all the lessons he had learned by this unfortunate event to produce needed self-perception and changes in his behaviour and his values. He came to himself.

Jesus used a dramatic story to portray human helplessness and the loneliness that may go with it (Luke 10.29-35). He showed how the response to this helplessness tends to be the divide that separates the mature from the immature. We usually call it the story of the Good Samaritan, but actually it is better understood as the three immature and the three mature persons whose personal development is measured by their response to the helpless person who becomes the yardstick for measuring their personal adequacy.

First, Jesus portrays the behaviour of those who seek to escape responsibility by trivial activity. These are the people who make excuses to avoid responsibility. What they were doing was not bad; it just was not good enough in the circumstances. First was the lawyer who used his legal skills and sophistry to try to avoid facing the basic question of responsibility. Like the ancient question, 'Am I my brother's keeper?', the lawyer wanted to retreat into semantics and definitions. He really knew who his neighbour was, but he wanted to avoid the burdensome meaning. Second was the priest who casually observed human need but wanted to get away from any messy obligations because he had to get to the synagogue and conduct services. So he used something good to avoid something better. The third person, a Levite, a custodian of sacred things, was more concerned, but still

129

avoided involvement by remembering that he had other important obligations. These three men represented the negative approach to human need.

Then Jesus illustrated three persons who 'responded to need. What courage it took to make the Samaritan the hero of the story, for the Samaritans were the outcasts, the socially unacceptable people. But the Samaritan showed compassion and ministered to the man's varied needs. He treated his wounds; he did not leave him in a dangerous and exposed condition, but used his own beast of burden to take the injured man to a safe place. Then he provided for his care until he was able again to care for himself. Second was the innkeeper who provided care and shelter for people without regard to race, colour or creed. Third was the person who had the bravery needed to confront a hostile group of people with a mirror to help them to see themselves and assess their own behaviour.

The seventh person in the story is unknown. We have no knowledge of the man who fell among thieves except that he was alone in threatening circumstances; his need was obvious, for he was helpless to care for himself. Yet this unknown person became the measure of all the other persons in this masterful little story. And even the lawyer who was so shamefaced that he would not even say the word 'Samaritan', got the point and admitted that the true neighbour was the one who ministered to the needy. The point of the story is summed up in two of the shortest words in our language. 'Go and do.'

The lonely, the broken, the desperate are there to test our ability to respond. The perspective that Jesus gives us is not obscure. It confronts us with our obligations to help and heal.

The last of these incidents that Jesus used to show our responsibility for breaking through the barriers that isolate and fracture life has to do with a woman who loved not wisely but too much (John 8.7). She was taken in the very act of adultery, breaking one of the Ten Commandments. But Jesus had a primary concern for people that moved beyond rules and prejudices. He knew that the Mosaic code had come out of a tradition which treated women as chattels, a lower form of creature who might be bought and sold, and over whom her masculine owner had power of life and death.

Any breaching of this ancient code made men feel uneasy. Their power and status was threatened by an effort to liberate women from this ancient past. But Jesus saw women as human beings first with a divine endowment, made in the image of God. It was secondary that they had some biological characteristics that separated them from men. He was not about to let this difference in endowment become a means of enslavement and death.

Those who created the conflicting situation wanted to get Jesus into a compromising position of challenging the Mosaic law, which was considered sacred. They would have been pleased to have him support them in their prejudicial judgment. But Jesus was concerned about something deeper. He would not support life-destroying behaviour either of the mob or of the woman who was accused. He lifted the basis for judgment to a higher level and again made them confront themselves. 'Let him without sin cast the first stone.' The stoning did not take place. A life was spared. A chance for redemption and change was substituted for petty thinking, violence and death.

In each of these lessons drawn from the example and teaching of Jesus we have reflected the biblical admonitions that support our concern for helping people beyond self-injuring behaviour, isolation and loneliness. It did not seem to make much difference to Jesus what the cause of the fractured relationship was. The important thing for him at each point was to move towards restoration, healing and redemption. This perception stands as a high point in the long human history of confronting isolation and loneliness, and sets the stage for our approach to creative understanding of the need for intimacy, identity and security.

13

Creative Solitude

There is a major difference between being lonely and being alone. One can be painful and the other the open door to glorious insights. Clark Moustakas makes the distinction clear when he says,

> Being alone without the explicit condition of loneliness is an act of conscious control, volition, thought and determination. Being alone is a necessary pause, being lonely is an ultimate condition. Being alone implies an evolution or continuity of experience, while being lonely means a total, radical change. Being alone is a way back to others. Being lonely is a way back to oneself.[1]

Each of us in our own way has experienced the pain of loneliness. We have also probably experienced those times when there was a great leap forward in our inner growth just because we were able to have a time alone, to think, to feel and to integrate experience.

When I finished college the final months had been filled with strenuous study, the writing of papers and the preparation for exams. When it was over I wanted to get away from everybody and everything to be alone for a while. I rented a cabin on a remote hillside where I could see no other habitation, carried up my bundles of food supplies and a few books. During that period of aloneness something wonderful went on. I had a chance to get acquainted with myself not as a struggling student but as a person with feelings and growing self-perceptions. The books I read during those days have remained clear in my memory, for the reading was unhurried and there was no examination to follow. The reading was for the growth of self. I read Herman Melville's *Moby Dick* and became part of the struggle against a mystical foe that challenged life's greatest effort. I read Lewis Mumford's life of

Herman Melville and gained a new appreciation of the function of biography in helping one to make new friends. I spent unhurried hours quietly thinking without any sense of indolence or guilt at not producing evidence of my industry. I was certainly alone, but it was a creative experience and there was no feeling of loneliness.

Some years later, when I was living in Greece, I went alone to the ruins of the temple of the mystery religion at Eleusis, twenty miles or so north of Athens. I went prepared to spend the night. The place was deserted, just a few of the stone columns still standing, but the large stone floor upon which the sacred rites of initiation were performed was still there. I sat down, leaning my back against the steps that surrounded the large space that must have been fifty or sixty yards square. Here in the quietness, lighted only by a moon that was nearly full and quite bright in the Mediterranean night, I let my mind ramble back through history to those scenes nearly twenty-five hundred years ago when early Greeks tried to find a meaning for life that could move beyond death, and a moral code that could guide them towards the behaviour worthy of eternal life. In that state of mind and in that place the consciousness moved beyond the boundaries of space and time and one became identified with the long and painful quest for meaning for life and for relationship with the source of life's meaning.

Some years after this, having developed a love for the mystical architecture of the thirteenth- and fourteenth-century Gothic cathedrals, I spent many hours travelling from one to another to let my soul breathe in the majesty and meaning of these heroic affirmations of faith and deep tribute to the quest for meaning through worship. I found a transforming experience in sitting before a magnificent window of stained glass that had been the teacher, guide and inspiration of millions of people through many centuries. When life tends to lose its perspective or become bogged down in routines that obscure the higher visions, I head back for renewal in my beloved cathedrals. Last spring I spent ten days going from one cathedral town to another in Normandy, Picardy and Brittany, worshipping alone. I would go quietly into the sacred place, find a spot with glorious perspectives on glass, sculpture and religious symbols, light a candle and pray and meditate until the candle had moved through its time-span, and darkness followed the light. During these times I would renew acquaintance, seek purification and let my consciousness grow in its perspectives of my place in a long and fruitful tradition. In Chartres I shared the pilgrimage of those who came from far and wide to be in the presence of their sacred ideal. At Mt St Michel I moved beyond my scientific orientation to commune with angels. At Rouen I felt the pangs of loneliness and pain as the recall of the spirit of Joan of Arc which permeated this place brought a sense of guilt to the tradition of which I was a part. In Arras I felt the tides of war and the ministry of peace, as in Cologne I felt the distress at acres of stained glass destroyed by warfare, and noble arches scarred by distructive impulses. And at Beauvais I sensed the human effort to stretch the material element of stone to its breaking point and still survive to give testimony to such daring. And all of this was done alone and in solitude that never lost its creative dimension.

In these sacred precincts I was able to enter into my deepest feelings and let the quiet tears soften my grief, the kinaesthetic pull of the arches lift my spirit, the noble concept of great worship speak to my soul's needs as the quietness seeped into my depth of being. On Pentecost Sunday I made my last visit to the long string of cathedrals for the service of praise and thanksgiving, that our spirits could be illuminated by great music, common bonds in worship beyond the barriers of language and nationality, and the questing spirit could find support among those who respected my aloneness as we managed to be alone and together at the same time.

Each of you in your own way can recall those moments in life where you experienced the benefits of creative aloneness. Perhaps a glorious sunrise or sunset where nature's beauty cried out for response, or a private time of communion in a church where you were a stranger but strangely not separated from those about you, or the time when you held a child in your arms and knew that you shared in the wonder of creation even though at times it seemed a lonely process. Being alone in the proper spirit can enrich life. And our Master was observed at the beginning of a day to go out into a lonely, desert place. We can be sure that he was alone with the source of inspiration that directed his life and made him what he was.

134

There has been an inclination in recent years to feel that being alone is unfortunate and unproductive. In our constant effort to be together in trivial activity we may have forgotten that being alone may be an important time for growth and personal integration. So we tend to become slaves of unproductive activities when there could be wise and helpful relationships if we had the courage to engage in creative solitude and the privileged chance to be alone with our best selves.

How can this be done? Several years ago I talked to a perceptive editor who said that every writer should have a committee with whom he is in constant communication. They might sit just beyond his desk so that he could be constantly aware of them. The committee should be made up of his grandmother and a teenager, a college professor and a truck driver, an atheist and a saint. When he writes so that he speaks clearly and convincingly to each of the members of his social committee all together at the same time, he knows his language is clear and easily understood.

This idea of writing for a committee suggested another form of committee that has enriched my life immeasurably. It is a committee of true friends. These people are carefully selected to support the needs of my growing spirit. The committee members can change from time to time as my needs and interests change, but they are always ready to serve me and guarantee that I am never alone, but always have the best companionship possible. The wonder of this committee is that they do not need to live nearby or even be physically alive in this century. But they are always there for consultation, and their spirits resonate with mine whenever I want to be with them.

My committee is made up of some remarkable people. There is Socrates, who was never afraid to ask the penetrating question, for he knew that we seldom get the right answers until we ask the right questions. Also there is St Francis, who responded to life with the warmth of an all-encompassing love. He felt a kinship with birds and beasts, with trees and flowers, with people in all stages of life and in all sorts of needs. He was free of prejudice and dominated by openness of spirit. So also I would have as a member of my committee John Wesley, who combined a remarkable brain and a strangely warmed spirit in a life that was so energized that almost single-handed he changed the course of English social, political and religious life. He had a clear sense of who he was and the purpose of his life, and so his direction was set. He wasted little energy in himself or in those others who accepted his leadership. I would also include Henry David Thoreau, who was able to establish a mystical relationship with nature and walk among trees, flowers, and hills as if they could communicate with him. The more he lived with and studied their lives, the more he found an inner security that reduced material preoccupations and enriched the spiritual meanings of existence. I would also like Simone Weil on my committee, for she found a complete devotion to human need as she discovered a complete identification with God's purpose for her life. When she wrote *Waiting on God*, she confirmed the meaning of a supreme identity and became one of the authentic saints of our century. This singleness of purpose she achieved by putting God first in life is a constant challenge. And I want Paul Robeson also to be on the committee, for he represents a largeness of personal courage, a sense of direction that fought constantly for the outcast and the oppressed, at the same time that he used his unusual endowment to make the world more beautiful with his music and his dramatic skill.

To be actively identified with a committee of such remarkable people is not only a constant challenge to life but also a guarantee that being alone will always be a creative experience. I can choose the people I want for my friends from the ancient past or the present, from every walk of life and every type of personality. They can be constantly there in the middle of a restless night, or when a time of testing comes. The individual always has the chance to share his times of being alone with the best people, the best literature, the best music, the best art and the best architecture that history has produced. And in addition he can live among the saints, and the finest revelation of the power of God to be at work in and through the human form. This, then, gives a different perspective on the human condition, and being alone with the best of history can make this aloneness the essence of true creativity.

But this kind of extended friendship calls for a major contribution on our part. We cannot merely appoint a distinguished committee to share our lives and be our friends. We must invest the energy and the attention that can make the relationship productive. How do we do that? Abraham Maslow tries to express this mood of moving with the appointed committee in these words:

> No blocks against the matter in hand means that we let it flow in upon us. We let it wreak its will upon us. We let it have its way. We let it be itself. Perhaps we can even approve of its being itself . . . a kind of trust in the self and a trust in the world which permits the temporary giving up of straining and striving, of volition and control, of conscious coping and effort. To permit oneself to be determined by the intrinsic nature of the matter-in-hand here-now.[2]

The friendship that always seeks control destroys much of the potential of the relationship, while the willingness to pay attention and rest comfortably in the relationship can nourish the soul in the quiet interchange of the deep awareness that changes our being.

Loneliness tends to be a retreat from relationship and is caused not so much by circumstances as by some inner fear. Erich Fromm speaks of the protective limits we place upon ourselves in order to avoid the obligations of friendship and creative relationships. 'We share the general phobia of being too close to a person, of penetrating through the surface to his core, and so we prefer to see little, no more than is necessary for our particular dealings with the other person.'[3] This limited, manipulative form of indifference to others is characteristic of a commercial culture. The salesman relates to the customer only at the point where he thinks it is necessary for his purpose of making a sale. But this limited form of relationship, when related to all of life, can create a society of sociopaths whose interest in others is to use them rather than relate to them. Then paying attention to another is so limited in purpose and method that it actually destroys the possibility of significant knowing of another. That is why so often in the process of marriage-counselling the salesman or the engineer is in trouble, for his main efforts in life are centred upon manipulation or exerting pressure. But another form of understanding and relationship is essential to inti-

137

macy and identification with another. This is a creative skill that can be learned in the times of loneliness when persons examine their lives and their relationships and grow into a new awareness of what they are like, what other people are like, and how this growth in understanding can build bridges rather than barriers. To quote Fromm again, 'Only as one has reached a degree of inner maturity which reduces projection and distortion to a minimum, can one experience creativity'.[4] Then the relationship is not limited to a thought, but becomes an experience of complete oneness with another.

As Simone Weil affirmed, the ability to achieve this complete state of oneness is rooted in a value-system that grows from an all-consuming effort to achieve the supreme identity by paying attention to God so completely that the human nature and the divine nature are one and inseparable. Then human creativity is fulfilled as we see it manifested so completely in the relationship of Jesus and his Lord. The unity of being unified life and gave it creative perspective. But this did not just happen. It was the end-result of great discipline and the willingness to move beyond the easy temptations to manipulate the material resources of life by changing molecular structure and turning stone into bread. It was further refined by the discipline that was shown in refusing to violate the laws of nature, even to be spectacular and gain attention. It was the determination of Jesus to work within the laws of nature that grounded his life in both the physical and the spiritual realities. And he lived beyond the temptation to make quick and easy compromises that destroyed integrity in the name of political expediency. The power to gain this discipline and mastery over life did not appear to come from political rallies, social functions or even from the study of manuals of ethics, but rather from the creative solitude in the lonely places where perspective was clear, responsibility uncomplicated and compromise with the ultimate realities of life impossible.

Alfred North Whitehead has claimed that the psychical is the creative advance into novelty. Edmund Sinnott has pointed out that the process of evolution at the biological level has been a long slow process, but that rapid advancement came about when the mind was engaged. Ralph Lillie went even further. 'Inertia is primarily a physical property, a

138

correlate of the conservation which is a recognized character of the physical as physical. In contrast, the psychical, being a faculty of novelty, is the anticonservative property of nature.'[5] In other words, mind is the source of creativity. Each of us has control over the function of our minds. We can think of one thing at a time. We can choose what we will hold in the focus of consciousness. We tend to become what we pay attention to in terms of our life's creative direction.

In his autobiography, Pablo Casals tells of a contrast in values that illustrates how we become what we pay attention to. A Fascist general of Franco affirmed that if he ever caught Casals, he would cut his arms off at the elbows and then would see what good his cello was. But when Casals came to town the democratic forces set up an impromptu concert and thousands of the Loyalists came together for a two-hour concert in the midst of their efforts to defend the city of Barcelona. The Fascist general's cry was 'Long Live death', and the Loyalist throngs cried 'Long live Casals'. What we pay attention to can either rot the inner being or glorify it.

A cosmos that is measured only in material terms is bound to cause the human spirit to feel diminished when it asks, 'In the midst of such tremendous space, what am I? How can I count for anything when I am a miserable creature on a third-rate planet spinning about one of the smaller of the ten billion suns in our personal galaxy? To try to give significance to my being in the midst of such vastness is folly indeed.' But a cosmology measured by statistics is quite a different one from that measured by emotions and meanings. 'What is man that thou are mindful of him, and the son of man that thou ministerest to him? For thou has made him little lower than the angels, and endowed him with wisdom and power.' This other cosmological picture is compatible with the scientific perceptions of our day, where consciousness-psychology and nuclear physics are giving a concept of man and nature that create the basis for a new and challenging theological synthesis.

The inner theology of the New Testament, the quest for and nurture of an inner kingdom of meaning, is now supplemented by a theology that emerges from the interaction of a concept of the human as the creature endowed with the capacity for God-consciousness and the ability to give meaning to the endowment that is bestowed on the human being. This consciousness has its highest manifestation in the ability to attribute cosmic meaning to the creation beyond the self that is the revelation of the God of law and order, wonder and mystery, personal in man and personalized through the revelation of Christ and all those who in the mind of Christ share in this meaning-creating process.

The ultimate of creativity is found, not in the words we speak or the symbolism of the art forms we use, but in the relationship we can create between creature and Creator, the within self and the beyond self. When this unity of being is discovered, the possibilities of existential loneliness are dissolved in the relationship that transcends all else in life.

The major difference between being lonely and being alone is in the quality of being that encounters the experiences of life. Being alone can be the time for consolidation and growth. It can be the time for the discovery of the self in relation to the beyond self. It can be the time for practising the self-love that produces the true identity that makes it possible to love others and to love God. It can be the time when true creativity engulfs life rather than being a symbolic act to try to get away from feelings of separation from life's meaning. It can be the time for purification when the hostile and destructive emotions can be freely worked through, and the therapeutic resources of life can be digested and integrated into the larger context of living. It can be the time for the extending of the boundaries of life beyond the need for self-protection to the possibility of self-giving. It can then be the point where we become more at home with the inner kingdom of being and the outer dimensions of cosmic relationship.

This capacity for creative solitude can be enriched by discovering and practising the arts of being alone and together at the same time, which is the heart of worship. This can be the point where we combine the skills of meditation and contemplation. In meditation we direct the mental activity towards goals of ever greater perception, and in contemplation we let the fruits of our meditation flow back into our souls. We can look at a sunset and use our mental powers to appreciate its colour and its intellectual meanings. But when we cease our thinking and let the sunset happen to us

140

as emotional experience, we gain another level of response to our capacity for consciousness.

When body with its sensory abilities, and mind with its capacity for attributing meaning, and consciousness with its ability to integrate the insights of body, mind and spirit are set free to fulfil their highest creative potential, we discover that being alone may be the ultimate time of growth, and when this power to be creatively alone is exercised we may discover that we need never be lonely again. Beyond all of the fads, the gurus and the misguided quests we are brought to the place where we feel quietly at ease with ourselves and the experiences of life that structure our external movement but touch our inner being only as we permit.

Recently I stood before the statue of Moses Maimonides in the Jewish enclave of Seville. I thought of the wisdom of this Jewish philosopher who lived eight hundred years ago. He speaks to our modern need to move beyond our existential loneliness by establishing clearly our link with God which can produce for us the relationship beyond all other relationships, and in so doing find the secret of all true communication within the self and with other selves. In his *Guide for the Perplexed*, he wrote:

I have shown you that the intellect which emanates from God unto us is the link that joins us to God. We have it in our power to strengthen that bond, if you chose to do so, or weaken it gradually till it breaks, if you prefer this. It will only become strong when you employ it in the love of God, and seek that love . . . You must know that even if you were the wisest man in respect to the true knowledge of God, you break the bond between you and God whenever you turn entirely your thoughts or attention to the necessary food or any necessary business; you are then not with God and He is not with you; for that relation between you and Him is actually interrupted in those moments . . . I will now commence to show you how to educate and train yourselves in order to attain that great perfection.

The wisdom of the philosopher, the discipline of the seeker, and the cosmic unity of the person who lives beyond existential loneliness is described as 'praying without ceasing', or 'being constant in prayer'. Here prayer is far more than an act or a string of verbal symbols. Rather it is the constant mood of life, that achieves the resonance that cannot be fractured, and the relationship that is closer than breathing and nearer than hands and feet.

Our day with its external values, its manipulative relationships and its materialistic measurement of worth, is sentenced to existential loneliness. But there are the powers within and the capacity for consciousness that can create new values, create new intimacies, and create a new sense of worth that can emerge when we take time to be quiet, develop the mood of listening, and achieve the fruits of creative solitude that can be the best antidote to an all-pervading loneliness that plagues our time.

Notes

Introduction

1. Doris Lessing, 'The Woman's Role', *Harper's Magazine*, June 1973.

2. Harry H. Sisler, 'Awareness', from *Starlight*, Storter Press, Gainsville, Florida 1975, p.54. This and the following extracts are used by permission of the author.

Chapter 2

1. Robert S. Weiss, *Loneliness. The Experience of Emotional and Social Isolation*, MIT Press, Cambridge, Mass. 1973.

Chapter 3

1. Page references are to Daniel Defoe, *Robinson Crusoe*, Everyman edition, Dent 1945.

Chapter 4

1. Karl Menninger, *The Crime of Punishment*, Viking Books, New York 1968.

2. Hornell Hart, *Autoconditioning*, Prentice-Hall, Englewood Cliffs, New Jersey 1956.

3. Earl A. Grollmann, *Talking about Divorce*, Beacon Press, Boston 1975.

Chapter 5

1. Richard E. Byrd, *Alone*, G.P. Putnam Sons, New York 1938.

2. Henry D. Thoreau, *Walden*, Tichnor and Fields, Boston 1854.

3. Flanders Dunbar, *Emotions and Bodily Changes*, Columbia University Press, New York 1954, p.535.

4. Martin Gumpert, *The Anatomy of Happiness*, McGraw-Hill, New York 1951, p.3.

5. James J. Lynch, *The Broken Heart. The Medical Consequences of Loneliness*, Basic Books, New York 1977, 75-7.

6. Geoffrey Gorer, *Death, Grief and Mourning*, Cresset Press 1965.

7. Rollo May, *The Meaning of Anxiety*, Ronald Press, New York 1950.

8. Lynch, *The Broken Heart*, p.78.

9. Ibid., p.79.

10. Ibid., p.80.

11. Ibid., p.81.

12. Ibid., p.81.

13. Lawrence LeShan, *You Can Fight For Your Life. Emotional Factors in the Causation of Cancer*, Evans, New York 1977, p.23.

14. Ibid., pp.23f.

15. Lynch, *The Broken Heart*, p.113.

16. Ibid., p.114.

17. Ibid., p.121.

18. Viktor Frankl, *From Death Camp to Extentialism*, Beacon Press, Boston 1959.

19. Lynch, *The Broken Heart*, p.132.

20. Ibid., p.150.

21. Erik H. Erikson, 'Identity and the Life Cycle', from *Psychological Issues*, Vol.1, No.1, International Universities Press, New York, pp.55-7.

22. Thomas Hackett and Avery Weisman, *Death and Identity*, edited by Robert L. Fulton, John Wiley & Sons, New York 1958, p. 254.

23. Lynch, *The Broken Heart*, pp.155, 36.

Chapter 6

1. Philippe Ariès, 'The Family and the City', *Daedalus*, Spring 1977, pp.227-35.

2. Henry Adams, *Mont Saint Michel and Chartres*, Houghton-Mifflin, Boston 1922.

3. Henry Adams, *The Education of Henry Adams*, Houghton-Mifflin, Boston 1918.

4. Victor Fuchs, *Who Shall Live? Health, Economics and Social Choice*, Basic Books, New York 1974, p.53.

5. Lynch, *The Broken Heart*, pp.7f.

6. Jacob Needleman, *A Sense of the Cosmos*, Doubleday 1975.

7. Dorothy Parker, *Sunset Gun*, Boni and Liveright, New

York 1941, p.20.

8. Rod McKuen, *Lonesome Cities*, Random House, New York 1968, pp.9, 93.

Chapter 7

1. Karl Menninger, *Man against Himself, and The Human Mind*, Alfred Knopf, New York 1949, p.128.

2. Karen Horney, *The Neurotic Personality of our Times*, W.W. Norton and Co., New York 1938.

3. Craig R. Eisenfrath, *The Unifying Moment*, Harvard University Press 1971, p.214.

4. Lewis Mumford, *The Condition of Man*, Secker and Warburg 1945, p. 290.

5. Jerry Greenwald, *Creative Intimacy*, Simon and Schuster, New York 1975.

Chapter 9

1. Harry H. Sisler, *Starlight*, p.6.

2. Emmett Holt, *The Care and Feeding of Children*, US Children's Bureau, Department of Health, Education and Welfare, Washington DC.

3. Ibid., pp.7f.

4. Edgar N. Jackson, *Understanding Prayer*, Hawthorn Books, New York 1968, reissued SCM Press 1980.

5. Erik Erikson, *Growth and Crises of the Healthy Personality*, International Universities Press 1959, pp.50-100.

6. Carl Jung, *Modern Man in Search of a Soul*, Routledge 1933.

Chapter 10

1. Charles Frankel, *The Case for Modern Man*, Beacon Press, Boston 1959, p.2.

2. Ibid., p.17.

3. Peter Berger et al., *The Homeless Mind*, Random House, New York 1973.

4. George Gilder, *Sexual Suicide*, The New York Times Books 1973, p.1.

5. Ibid., p.1.

6. Ibid., p.4.

7. Edmund Sinnott, *The Biology of the Spirit, Cell and Psyche, Two Roads to Truth*, Viking Books, New York 1953; Pierre

Teilhard de Chardin, *The Future of Man*, Collins 1964; *The Phenomenon of Man*, Collins 1969.

8. Gilder, *Sexual Suicide*, p.237.

9. Ibid., p.242.

Chapter 11

1. Ignace Lepp, *The Depths of the Soul*, Doubleday, Garden City, New York 1967, pp.61, 50f.

2. Harry Sisler, *Starlight*, p.5.

3. Ibid., p.15

4. Dr Enrico Fermi pioneered research on atomic particles and ushered in the nuclear age when he first split the nucleus of the uranium atom and built the first nuclear reactor in 1942. Probably one of the dozen or so leading scientists of this century, he made practical the theoretical findings of Albert Einstein.

5. Joseph Campbell, *Myths to Live By*, Bantam Books, New York 1973.

6. Ignaz Semmelweiss, a Hungarian doctor (1818-65), first related the germ theory to body infections by his study of childbirth fever. Hounded to death by colleagues who rejected his theories, he later had an important influence on medical practice through his writings.

7. W. Irwin Thompson, *At the Edge of History*, Harper and Row 1971.

8. Max Planck, *Scientific Autobiography*, Philosophical Library, New York 1949.

9. Rollo May, *Man's Search for Himself*, Norton, New York 1953, p.14.

10. Ibid., p.26.

Chapter 13

1. Clark Moustakas, *Loneliness and Love*, Prentice-Hall, Englewood Cliffs, New Jersey 1972, p.22.

2. Abraham Maslow, *The Farther Reaches of Human Nature*, Viking Books, New York 1971, p.67.

3. Harold Anderson (ed.), *Creativity and its Cultivation*, Harper, New York 1959, p.7.

4. Ibid., p.46.

5. Ibid., p.12.